IMPLEMENTING SCHOOL-BASED MANAGEMENT:

Insights into Decentralization from Science and Mathematics Departments

URBAN INSTITUTE REPORT 93-4

Harry P. Hatry,
Elaine Morley,
Brenda Ashford, and
Timothy M. Wyatt

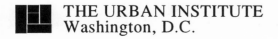

THE URBAN INSTITUTE
Washington, D.C.

Library of Congress Cataloging in Publication Data

Implementing School-Based Management: Insights into Decentralization from Science and Mathematics Departments / Harry P. Hatry. . . [et al.].

1. School-based management—United States. 2. Schools—United States—decentralization. 3. Science—study and teaching (Secondary)—United States. 4. Mathematics—Study and teaching (Secondary)—United States. I. Hatry, Harry P. II. Series.

LB2806.35.I47   1994   93-35809
371.2—dc20   CIP

(Urban Institute Report 93-4, ISSN 0897-7399)

ISBN 0-87766-612-1 (paper)
ISBN 0-87766-611-3 (cloth)

Printed in the United States of America

Distributed by University Press of America
4720 Boston Way   3 Henrietta Street
Lanham, MD 20706   London WC2E 8LU
                         ENGLAND

THE URBAN INSTITUTE REPORTS

are designed to provide rapid dissemination of research and policy findings. Each report contains timely information and is rigorously reviewed to uphold the highest standards of policy research and analysis.

The Urban Institute is a nonprofit policy research and educational organization established in Washington, D.C., in 1968. Its staff investigates the social and economic problems confronting the nation and government policies and programs designed to alleviate them. The Institute disseminates significant findings of its research through the publications program of its Press. The goals of the Institute are to sharpen thinking about societal problems and efforts to solve them, improve government decisions and performance, and increase citizen awareness of important policy choices.

Through work that ranges from broad conceptual studies to administrative and technical assistance, Institute researchers contribute to the stock of knowledge available to guide decision making in the public interest.

Conclusions or opinions expressed in Institute publications are those of the authors and do not necessarily reflect the views of staff members, officers or trustees of the Institute, advisory groups, or any organizations that provide financial support to the Institute.

Acknowledgments

The authors thank the 12 school districts and 19 schools within those districts that participated in this effort. Each gave us excellent cooperation in setting up needed interviews and providing documents related to their school-based management efforts. The principals, science and mathematics department heads, and teachers gave generously of their time. Most districts also reviewed their sections of our draft report and suggested modifications. We particularly wish to thank the following persons at the seven school districts who worked with us to schedule our on-site visits: Dee Foster, Dade County, Florida; Dan Tosado, Albuquerque, New Mexico; Marilyn Wittner, Hillsborough County, Florida; Anne McKown, Prince George's County, Maryland; Den Boyd, Prince William County, Virginia; Dolores Riley, Salt Lake City, Utah; and Eleanor Ortiz, Santa Fe, New Mexico.

A number of interns provided considerable help on various phases of the work. Andrew Draheim and Chris Dumler of Michigan State University, Hilary Christensen of Sioux Falls College, and Jonathan Stanger of Georgetown University helped substantially at beginning of the study, and Jonathan provided highly useful assistance on the preparation of the final report. Bruce Barnett and Elizabeth Matthews of Yale University and Megan Hunter of Michigan State University also assisted us briefly at other times.

We also wish to thank Betty Malen, Educational Leadership and Policy Studies, University of Washington, and Paula White, Center for Policy Research in Education, University of Wisconsin/Madison, for their suggestions and advice early in the project, and Sophie Sa of the Panasonic Foundation for suggestions regarding field visit candidates.

We are very indebted to J. David Lockard, professor of biology and director of the International Clearinghouse for the Advancement of Science Teaching at the University of Maryland/College Park, and to Harris S. Shultz, professor of mathematics at California State University/Fullerton, for their valuable technical assistance. They reviewed our plan of action, draft interview guides, and draft final report, providing very helpful suggestions.

Finally, we are very grateful to the Studies and Indicators Program under the Education and Human Resources Directorate of the National Science Foundation and to the GTE Foundation for their financial support. Of course, the views expressed throughout this report are those of the authors and do not necessarily represent those of either foundation or the Urban Institute.

Contents

PART ONE

Implementation Issues

PART THREE
Overall Findings and Recommendations

Appendices

Abstract

This report presents the findings and recommendations of an examination of the implementation of a major form of decentralization, school-based management (SBM). It is based on case studies of science and mathematics departments of 10 high schools and 9 middle or junior high schools, in 12 school systems.

The study found that implementation often falls short of the ideal. It did not find dramatic changes resulting from SBM. However, those schools and faculty members that took advantage of their added flexibility under SBM were able to achieve numerous small-scale improvements.

The report provides a series of recommendations for school districts and individual schools to increase the likelihood of successful implementation of decentralization efforts such as SBM. The findings and recommendations cover such issues as: the extent of decentralization of budgeting expenditure and personnel decisions, the role of site councils and department heads, and communication and training needs.

Executive Summary

This report presents the findings and recommendations of study of implementation of a major form of decentralization, school-based management (SBM) in middle, junior high, and high schools. The purpose is to provide insights that help school district and school administrators and department heads make decentralization decisions. The findings and recommendations herein are based primarily on the perspectives of science and mathematics faculty. However, since SBM is implemented school-wide, most of them also apply to implementation of SBM across the board.

The report encompasses any activity that involves decentralization, whether or not a school or school district has labeled it SBM. A case study approach was applied to 10 high schools and 9 middle or junior high schools in 12 school systems, across the United States all of which had at least two years of experience implementing a decentralization process. We made in-person site visits to two schools in each of 7 school districts, reviewed school documents, and conducted in-depth telephone interviews to relevant personnel in the remaining 5 districts.

FINDINGS

There was little opposition to decentralization principles in either the literature or in interview responses. Implementation of those principles, however, often fell far short of ideal, raising the question of whether SBM can be adequately implemented under current structural and financial school system conditions.

There were many noteworthy examples of improvements in science and mathematics education, although success in introducing changes varied considerably. For the most part, SBM efforts did not appear to be focused on improving education outcomes.

A common problem was confusion about roles and responsibilities. The extent to which the principal shared decision making and encouraged faculty to make suggestions was critical. Inadequate communication among school administrators, staff, and the site council on SBM-related issues was another major problem. Nor was parent and student involvement perceived to have had much impact, although most interviewees believed it to be desirable.

The most frequent substantive new delegation of responsibility by the school district to individual schools under SBM was greater control over their own budgets, which appears to have been widely used. Within·the schools, budgeting responsibility was usually further delegated to the department heads, who in turn sought input from faculty members.

While site councils play a major role in descriptive literature about SBM, they were often not a very effective player in the schools we examined.

Teachers often complained about SBM but wanted more. They liked the increased input into decisions but did not think SBM was working as well as it should, and felt burdened by the extra hours entailed.

This report provides a series of recommendations for school districts and individual schools to increase the likelihood of successful implementation of decentralization efforts such as SBM. The findings and recommendations cover such issues as: extent of decentralization of budgeting, expenditures, and personnel decisions; the roles of site councils, department heads, and district-level staff specialists; and communication and training needs.

SELECTED RECOMMENDATIONS

1. Application of SBM management approaches should continue. We found enough achievements to warrant continued effort.

2. SBM should be introduced into schools *with* principals able and willing to delegate responsibility. Other principals should be given assistance in assuming a participatory rather than authoritarian role.

3. Delegation should not stay at the school level. It should be carried down through departments to individual faculty, giving them added flexibility relating to acquisition of supplies and equipment, participation in course scheduling, and content matters as well as instructional practices.

4. The school district should provide a forum for the interchange of information among schools about new actions and new teaching approaches.

5. The school district should assign district-level science and mathematics specialists to disseminate information on new technologies and training opportunities, provide technical assistance, undertake evaluations of major innovations introduced by faculty in district schools, and survey faculty

periodically for ways to improve the usefulness of the specialist services.

6. A school district and each implementing school should clearly communicate roles and responsibilities of different actors, including specifying continuing areas of uncertainty.

7. Each school should provide adequate two-way communication among actors at all levels, including teachers, department heads, the site council, and school administrators.

8. Schools and department heads should strongly encourage faculty to try new education approaches; however, faculty should not be forced into an "ideal" mold. SBM should not penalize individuality.

9. School districts, individual schools, and site councils should place more emphasis on tracking changes and their impact on student outcomes.

Although we did not find dramatic changes, numerous small-scale improvements did occur in schools, especially with faculty who took advantage of the added flexibility provided by decentralization. The concepts of SBM seem sound; successful implementation is hard. It will help if SBM is phased out as a label and decentralization becomes perceived by schools and faculty as "business as usual."

CHAPTER 1

Introduction and Scope

This report presents the findings and recommendations of a study of the implementation of a major form of decentralization, school-based management (SBM), particularly with respect to science and mathematics education in the middle/junior high and high schools.

Our purpose is to provide school administrators (at both the district and school levels) and science and mathematics department heads with insights that might help them make their own decisions about decentralization approaches such as SBM. We also hope this material will be useful to those already implementing some version of SBM.

The findings are based primarily on the perspectives of science and mathematics faculty. Our goal was to ascertain how SBM has been implemented, what problems have arisen, what has helped implementation, and the effects of the SBM process on science and mathematics education. We did not attempt to evaluate the impact of SBM on student learning; however, we did explore the extent to which SBM affected science and mathematics educational practices.

Since SBM is implemented school-wide, not just in individual departments, most of the findings and recommendations presented here are also likely to apply to implementation of SBM "across-the-board."

CURRENT INTEREST IN DECENTRALIZATION AND SCHOOL-BASED MANAGEMENT

In recent years, Americans have come to perceive our elementary and secondary education as a major problem. Science and mathematics education, in particular, is the focus of considerable concern because of the perceived importance of these subjects to economic progress and the reported gaps in achievement between U.S. students and students of other developed countries. As a result, there has been an extraordinary number of efforts to improve education in these areas.

One common and widely implemented reform initiative has been to give more authority and responsibility to individual schools and their staffs. Across the nation educators have begun to experiment with increasing school-level authority, usually under the label of "school-based management" (SBM) or some variation such as "school-based decision making," or "site-based management." These efforts have taken numerous forms, with countless variations in *what responsibilities and authority* are actually delegated, *to whom* they are delegated, and *what specific processes and procedures are used.*

SBM is similar to other major movements toward "participatory management" in which all employees of an organization are solicited for input and participation into decision making. Total Quality Management (TQM) is probably the most common such approach currently used in the public and private sectors. As of this writing, an increasing number of states and school districts are experimenting with TQM, as is the federal government. TQM's "empowerment" of all employees, continuous attention to quality improvement, emphasis on teams, and concern with the customer are all quite compatible with—and major features desired of—SBM-type approaches.

The basic assumption of school-based management is the same as that of decentralization in general, namely that personnel at the point of service delivery, i.e., individual schools, are better able to identify specific problems and needs of their own students and schools. Thus, they should be given the authority, responsibility, and opportunity to alter procedures and practices to meet these needs. This added leeway and flexibility, it is further hypothesized, should better stimulate and unleash school personnel to improve their ability to educate and motivate students, and enable them to introduce new ideas more rapidly—including innovations in science and mathematics teaching—to better match the needs of their own students. It is further assumed that SBM will encourage the development and implementation of new ways of educating students—ways that might meet resistance if imposed from the outside.

On the negative side, processes such as SBM can have drawbacks, as noted in previous studies of SBM. For example, SBM can require considerable time and effort from some school staff. Cooperative decision-making procedures can delay the decision-making process, and many staff may not like the additional time requirements, or the added responsibility, or other aspects of the revised decision-making process (such as school-site councils). Further, lack of clarity as to what SBM is, how it is to be implemented, and who can do what can confuse school personnel and engender dissatisfaction.

In the literature review presented in appendix B to this report, we discuss in more detail the general theory of school-based management and past research findings on SBM. Our report focuses on the practical implications of decentralization and SBM on science and mathematics education as found in the school districts and schools that we examined.

DEFINITION AND SCOPE OF SBM USED IN THIS REPORT

Each school district we examined has its own version of school-based management. Some districts apply rather narrow definitions of SBM, such as giving individual schools added budget authority. Other school systems go much further in their decentralization, transferring to schools a wide spectrum of responsibilities and opportunities for staff input concerning use of funds, procurement, curriculum alterations, instructional procedures and processes, and personnel matters. The three primary decision-making areas decentralized under SBM are budgeting, curriculum and instruction, and personnel.

This report encompasses any activity that involves decentralization, whether or not a school or school district has labeled it "SBM." For example, if a school district permitted individual schools and their science and mathematics departments to purchase supplies and equipment previous to the district's formal SBM activity, we counted this under the broader topic of decentralizing science and mathematics education activities. Another example is "teaching teams," which have become common in middle schools. Because these teams usually are given considerable leeway in many aspects of their students' education, we consider such teams as a form of decentralization and have included them in our examination, even though they may have been implemented independent of SBM.

The implications of decentralization and SBM for science and mathematics departments and education cannot be assessed separately from the SBM environment as a whole in the school system and individual schools. Thus, while our examination is aimed at science and mathematics personnel at the school-site level, we have also looked at the district- and overall school-level SBM processes, albeit to a much lesser extent. As a result, some issues important to a full examination of decentralization and SBM implementation are not covered in depth because they do not appear specific to science and mathematics concerns. These include the role played by school boards in introducing SBM, participation of teacher associations/unions, factors responsible for initiating SBM processes in the first place, and district-level organization relating to SMB (though the role of district-level science and mathematics curriculum staff vis-à-vis SBM is discussed in one of our chapters).

We excluded elementary schools from our examination for two reasons: Our resources were limited, and extracting science- and mathematics-specific findings in elementary schools would be difficult since one teacher generally covers science, mathematics, and other core subjects.

EXTENT OF SHARED DECISION MAKING WITHIN THE SCHOOL

One element we have paid particular attention to is the extent to which various types of decisions have been decentralized *within the school building*. In some situations, decision-making authority may have been delegated primarily to the principal and no further, while in other schools, the department heads may be major partners, or individual faculty may play major roles. In some schools, some form of faculty council is the dominant force and the rest of the faculty is not substantially involved. Since SBM is being promoted under the theory that the persons delivering the services should be given as much initiative as possible; presumably individual faculty members should play major roles.

Similarly, a major issue in describing SBM efforts is to distinguish whether each category of school personnel (principals, site council members, department heads, and individual faculty members) plays a decision-making role or solely an advisory role. If the role is advisory, are the suggestions usually accepted? School districts with SBM usually delegate some additional authority (such as budget) to the school. Does the principal in turn delegate such authority to the council or to departments? Our findings discuss who participated, how significantly, and in what types of decisions.

The role of *parents* is also often emphasized as being important in SBM. Similarly, *student* input is often mentioned as an element of SBM. Our findings address these roles also.

STUDY METHODOLOGY

For this study, we used a case study approach. Between August 1991 and June 1992 we examined 12 school systems and 19 individual schools within those systems, comprising 10 high schools and 9 middle or junior high schools. We made on-site, in-person visits to two schools in each of seven of these school districts, for a total of 14 schools visited. We covered the remaining five school districts through review of written materials provided by them and extensive telephone interviews with personnel from the district office and from one school in each district.

We began this work assuming that the school district would be the basic unit of analysis. However, after our first set of field interviews (we used the first school district as our pilot site to test our interview guides and procedures), we found that individual schools within a school district could differ markedly. This pattern was repeated throughout our work: in effect, each school in a district represented a substantially different situation. For this reason, we consider the basic unit of analysis for this report to be the individual school building. Nevertheless, as will be seen, some of our findings also pertain to district-level issues.

We used two-person teams over three days for most on-site field visits. One day was spent at a middle/junior high school and one day at a high school. We typically spent the third day at the central district office interviewing personnel knowledgeable about the district's overall SBM effort as well as the science and mathematics curriculum specialists/supervisors. At the schools, the team members usually interviewed the principal and/or an assistant principal, the science and mathematics department heads, and members of the science and mathematics faculties. Most of the interviews were one-on-one. We also held one or more group meetings with science and mathematics faculties at each school. At some schools, particularly the smaller ones, we met with most, if not all, science and mathematics faculty.

For the school districts investigated by telephone interview, we typically spoke to two or three central district personnel, including one science or mathematics curriculum specialist/supervisor. We then held telephone interviews with staff from one school, including the principal, the science and mathematics department heads, and one teacher each in the science and mathematics departments. By phone or in person, we interviewed an average of more than 10 staff members per school. Overall, we spoke to 253 persons, comprising 88 science teachers; 86 mathematics teachers (including 19 science and 19 mathematics department heads); 25 principals and assistant principals; and 54 persons at the central district level, including 12 science or mathematics specialists, 12 superintendent or assistant superintendents, and 30 other persons, such as district SBM coordinators and specialists in budgeting and purchasing.

For their interviews the teams used a basic set of primarily open-ended questions, somewhat modified for each category of respondent (e.g., teachers, department heads, principals, district-level personnel, etc.). Interviews by telephone typically lasted 60 to 90 minutes. The on-site interviews varied from approximately 45 to 90 minutes. (Telephone interviews with teachers usually were conducted after school hours and therefore were not limited by the school bells, as were some of our on-site interviews.) On-site interviews with faculty sometimes were affected by the length of class periods, though many of those interviewed were able to give us extra time, in some instances because the principal had arranged for coverage of their classes.

Of the 186 science or mathematics personnel we interviewed (including department heads), all but 12 were currently teaching at the time of the interviews. The remainder were administrative personnel from the school or district offices. We did not have the resources to corroborate the findings with faculty from other departments or with faculty from other schools—either those with or without SBM. However, since information and opinions were obtained from numerous individuals in the same site, to some extent, the information was corroborated by the other respondents. In some cases, factual information was corroborated by written materials obtained at the relevant site.

We believe that, for the most part, responses to us were frank and candid, as indicated by the many negatives we heard about various aspects of the SBM process, and the very strong views expressed by some individuals interviewed. SBM is not a topic that appears to reflect highly on respondents' own careers, so there is little reason to expect deliberately skewed responses.

Selection of School Districts and Individual Schools

The 12 school districts we examined were selected from the group determined to have at least two years experience in implementing a SBM process (based on prior literature search and preliminary telephone interviews with persons with SBM experience, such as university researchers and foundations that had funded SBM efforts). Before finalizing selection of the school districts, we conducted at least one telephone interview with an official of each district to verify that the SBM effort had indeed been in place (and was not just in a planning phase) for approximately two years and that the district appeared to have delegated some real authority to at least one or more schools in the system.

The specific schools examined in each district were chosen by our district SBM contacts. Selections were based primarily on length of SBM experience and on the contact's perception that the schools were undertaking substantial SBM efforts.

Thus, the schools in this study tend to be those that are making the more intensive efforts to implement some form of SBM. They are not statistically representative of schools trying SBM across the country.

The Causality Issue

Our project design precluded any attempt to estimate in a substantive way the *impact* of SBM on student learning and interest in science and mathematics. Funds were not available, and even if they had been, this would be an extremely difficult and complex undertaking. Rather, we focused on "intermediate" outcomes, the changes that occurred in terms of who did what, including the *actual* changes in educational practices that took place. We did seek information in our interviews on impacts on students; these findings are reported in chapter 14. However, the project design and resources did not permit an in-depth examination of the extent to which school-based management itself had caused either these outcomes or the changes in educational practices we found.

Complicating this situation, science and mathematics education has also been undergoing major changes, if not upheavals, through such efforts as the National Council of Teachers of Mathematics' development of standards for mathematics and similar efforts by the National Science Teachers Association. Changes in curriculum content, the way material is taught, the teaching technology available, and testing practices being adopted by many state and local school districts have impacted on classroom practice in many schools.

We were not able to interview personnel from schools or school districts which had *not* instituted significant decentralization of responsibility. Nor were we able to interview faculty from disciplines other than science and mathematics to assess more directly whether science and mathematics faculty were affected differently than other faculty.

While we did not have information from such comparison groups, in many cases we felt that we had sufficient evidence to indicate that activities identified would not have occurred without the SBM initiative—or at the very least that school-based management had led to a significantly *earlier* introduction of these changes.

Special Circumstances of Each School

As one would expect, each school we examined had its own unique characteristics, including its own demographic factors, locational characteristics, and individual management styles and approaches, procedures regarding who provided input to various school decisions, and its own starting point in terms of current science and mathematics teaching practices. Thus, some of our examples of procedures and practices may appear to be old hat to some readers of this report, while for those particular schools they are new and advanced, and represent real progress for them. Each school needs to be evaluated in terms of its own starting point and the progress it has made.

REPORT ORGANIZATION

P art I of this report (chapters 2 to 10) focuses on the process of SBM and how it has changed various school activities. Chapters 2 and 3, respectively, describe our findings concerning the extent of decentralization of financial and personnel decisions in the schools investigated. Chapters 4, 5, and 6 discuss the roles of three major players in SBM: site councils, science and mathematics department heads, and parents. (We do not have separate chapters on the roles of principals and teachers, but these roles are discussed throughout the report.) Chapters 7 and 8 examine two major issues for SBM: school communications and training needs. Chapter 9 highlights differences between middle and high school levels, while chapter 10 addresses the role of school district-level science and mathematics personnel under a SBM system.

Part II (chapters 11 to 14) addresses the effects of SBM— those on teacher morale and job satisfaction (chapter 11), the accountability system for teachers and principals (chapter 12), science and mathematics teachers' instructional practices (chapter 13), and what we found about likely impacts on the students themselves (chapter 14). Each of chapters 2 through 14 contains detailed recommendations relevant to that chapter's subject matter.

Part III, comprising the final two chapters, provides overall findings and suggestions. Chapter 15 presents suggestions made by the school and district staff we interviewed. Chapter 16 presents our own judgments on the major findings and recommendations that emerge from the work.

Appendix A is a list of the schools and school districts we examined for this study, along with selected descriptive characteristics. Appendix B contains a review of the literature relating to school-based management and school restructuring that focuses on decentralization issues. That review was prepared at the beginning of our work and has undergone only minor updating since. However, it appears to capture much of the current thinking on SBM and is consistent with our basic findings. In this report, however, we explore some issues in considerably more detail than that found in most of the literature and discuss the specific application of SBM elements to science and mathematics departments.

In presenting examples in the report, for simplicity, we generally identify the school district and school level (e.g., high school or middle/junior high) without identifying the particular school. See appendix A for the individual schools.

PART ONE

Implementation Issues

CHAPTER 2

Extent of Decentralization of Budgeting and Expenditure Decisions

Permitting individual schools to budget and spend dollars as they see fit is a major element of school system decentralization. Funding decisions underpin many other decisions. The assumption is that those at the school building level can best determine the needs for their facilities, staff, and students and, therefore, should be free to apply resources to meet their individual needs.

Expenditure issues include not only how to develop the school budget, but also how to allocate (or reallocate) the school's funds (e.g., making transfers across different budget categories), and how to make procurement decisions. Schools commonly receive funds from a variety of sources, with different constraints imposed according to the source. For example, federal and state funds must often be used only for specific purposes and cannot be blended with the general-purpose budget.

Delegation of budgeting and expenditure control poses potential problems. Allowing each school unlimited flexibility in how to pay its faculty, for example, would likely raise major equity and fairness questions among schools in the district and could conflict with teacher association agreements. Allowing each school to select vendors for supplies and equipment could be detrimental to the district's ability to obtain large-quantity discounts. In addition, less experienced, untrained school personnel might make procurement errors that centralized procurement staff would not.

FINDINGS

Budget and expenditure flexibility were the responsibilities most commonly delegated to the school level. Some school districts extended budget authorities to schools in several phases (i.e., selected schools were initially given more budget authority on a pilot basis, with more schools added in later years). In some districts, schools had the option to apply for additional budgetary authority after the pilot phase.

A commonly used budget process is illustrated by an example from Albuquerque, New Mexico. Albuquerque schools developed their own budgets by modifying a projected budget distributed by the school district. The district budget office provided each school with estimated amounts for various budget categories based on projected enrollment, required pupil/teacher ratios, and so on. Schools used these estimates and instructions provided by the district budget office to develop proposed budgets. As part of this process, they were able to transfer funds among line items defined by the district as discretionary accounts, such as substitute teachers, supplies, equipment, and travel. Resulting school budgets were subject to approval by the district.

Budgetary decision making at the school level was handled by the school districts we examined in a variety of ways. The principal and the site council were the main budgetary actors in most schools, although some schools had special budget committees. (Site councils undertake a range of decision-making or advisory activities at the school. They are a distinguishing feature of SBM, and the subject of chapter 4.) One middle school had a separate technology committee to make decisions on spending technology funds, which were a separate allocation from the school district.

No district allowed its individual schools to deviate from district-wide salary scales. However, schools were usually allowed to provide extra payments to faculty for added activities that the faculty had often recommended, such as special tutoring services. We did not identify any schools that used their added budget flexibility to support a teacher merit-pay system for staff within the school (though conceivably this could be done with the consent of the teacher association).

In general, individual school flexibility over personnel costs was highly constrained by school district policies (and often teacher association agreements), such as maximum student/teacher ratios. However, some flexibility "around the edges" was usually available.

Budget Allocations Departments. Most schools allocated budgets to individual departments and sometimes to teaching teams. These budgets were typically for discretionary accounts, such as supplies and other instructional expenses, but not for staff. Teaching teams in some schools generally received small budgets for supplies or student-related expenses such as field trips and "rewards." However, we found that individual science or mathematics faculty members in some districts were unaware of the amount of their department (or team) budget.

Prince William County, Virginia, decentralized even more budget development authority to schools. The district calculated the total amount for each school for the year, and schools decided how much to allocate to each department and each cost category. Schools could make tradeoffs as long as they stayed within maximum pupil/teacher ratios.

Transfers among Accounts. A number of schools were able to make transfers among budget accounts, although restrictions were sometimes placed on which accounts or the amounts involved. For example, the Albuquerque school district identified "discretionary" accounts among which transfers could be made. Ability to transfer funds is related to another feature that science and mathematics personnel found attractive—the flexibility to modify spending decisions throughout the year, rather than being locked into the initial budget developed before the beginning of the fall term. Schools were usually not allowed to remove teachers and transfer personnel funds into other uses. However, in several districts, schools could make such transfers when a vacancy occurred.

In a Prince George's County, Maryland, middle school, the site council (which included all department heads) could agree to transfer funds among departments, as long as personnel allocations were not involved. For example, one year both the science and mathematics departments needed additional funds to replace lost or damaged texts. The site council reallocated funds from the foreign language department for this purpose. Transfers were made with the general understanding that those who gave up funds one year would benefit from transfers in the future.

Santa Fe, New Mexico, decentralized budgetary authority by allowing schools to transfer funds among a selected group of line items: supplies, staff development, and texts. These accounts were chosen because they were fairly easy to monitor by the school district, any errors would be relatively easy to correct, and staff sizes and salaries would not be affected.

In some places school district approval was required for transfers among accounts, involving paperwork and delays. This was reported as a source of frustration by some school personnel.

Instead of enabling transfers, Salt Lake City, Utah, combined selected budget categories, such as texts, supplies, periodicals, audiovisuals, etc., into one operating expenses category. This provided schools with more flexibility in spending without the necessity of transferring funds among categories.

Procurement Decisions. Many science and mathematics teachers indicated they felt they (or their departments) were better off under decentralized budgeting in terms of getting equipment or supplies that they wanted. In addition to added department responsibility and flexibility in allocating procurement dollars, decentralization simplified procedures for obtaining equipment and supplies in some schools. Science teachers in one school noted that the ability to make local purchases enabled them to do minor things that improved morale, such as repairing doors that had come off their hinges. The mathematics department head in one high school noted that departments had more flexibility in deciding how funds were spent under SBM, and some departments pooled resources to purchase supplies or equipment. The principal of one high school suggested it was not only faster, but more efficient (an important issue in periods of budget constraints) to have department heads deal directly with suppliers than to funnel paperwork through the school district's central office.

A high school in one district initiated joint department purchasing under decentralization to reduce duplication of equipment purchases. For example, the mathematics and science departments collaborated to purchase software that could be used by both departments.

In another high school, the science and mathematics departments structured their budgets to increase purchases of mathematics and science-related equipment and supplies, such as calculators, microscopes, and laboratory supplies. They used discretionary and instructional funds to purchase computers for their departments.

Some science and mathematics teachers indicated an interest in being able to contract for purchases and repairs at the departmental level. However, the teachers noted that "shopping around" for better prices was time consuming. Science and mathematics teachers in other schools felt they could buy equipment and supplies of better quality or more cheaply than the district's central purchasing unit. They requested a waiver to procure locally when they could obtain an item of equal quality but at a lower price than indicated on the district's list.

In those few locations where science and mathematics faculty made their own purchases, the transactions appeared to have been handled satisfactorily, despite the teachers' lack of procurement experience.

Special Purpose Funds. In Salt Lake City, schools could have the district pay for the cost of substitute teachers directly, or receive an allocation based on historical costs. Schools choosing the latter option managed their own substitute budget and used any excess funds not needed for substitutes to hire extra aides, secretaries, or teachers. If the school overspent the account, it had to take the additional funds from other accounts, except in cases of long-term illness where the district took the responsibility for funding substitutes. About half the schools in the district opted for this site-based substitute program.

Also in Salt Lake City the district provided each school with a special discretionary school improvement budget, allocated on a per pupil and per school basis, to promote activities included in school improvement plans. Principals were encouraged to get site council approval for expenditure of these funds and were required to keep school staff informed as to the amount received and how it was spent. Each school also received a discretionary equipment fund, which could be used only for items on a "standard list."

One junior high school in Hillsborough County, Florida, made a school-based decision to use SBM-related grant funds received from a private foundation to develop a dropout prevention program.

Ability to Carry Over Funds. Usually, schools were not given the authority to carry over unspent funds to future school years. Salt Lake City was an exception. According to district administrators, school spending patterns depend on the personality of the principal. Some principals spend almost everything they receive in one year, others hoard, and some do long-range planning. Dade County, Florida, schools were allowed to carry over funds, but only subject to annual school board approval (which had thus far been given). In Prince William County, schools could carry over up to $2,000. In Poway, California, schools were allowed to carry over 100 percent of their unspent instructional funds, and a percentage of staff units; the superintendent reported that principals felt this authority was one of the most empowering features of the district's SBM model.

In districts that did not allow carryovers, some science and mathematics faculty, department heads in particular, felt they had to spend the year's allocation—even unnecessarily—before it was lost forever.

Staff Time and Information Needs. Decentralization of budgeting authority implies that school personnel will take on additional, often unfamiliar, responsibilities. Central personnel in one district noted that the financial responsibilities of principals increased significantly under SBM. New responsibilities of principals included holding budget-related meetings, monitoring and tracking the budget, and doing long-range funding planning. Some principals (particularly longstanding ones) had problems understanding and coping with the new levels of financial responsibility. The central budget director in another district also noted that its principals had few financial skills (because the district had been highly centralized for 20 years).

Some principals, science and mathematics department heads, and faculty also commented on the problems of taking on additional budget responsibilities or questioned the value of doing so. The principal of one middle school noted that he was reluctant to seek additional budgetary authority for the school because of the paperwork involved, and since there would not be "much money to move around," the school would not gain much by having the additional authority. The principal of a high school in the same district indicated that he was not seeking more budget authority for the school because he felt the site council and faculty lacked the budgeting and accounting skills to make effective budget decisions or to take on more budgetary responsibility.

Some science and mathematics teachers felt they lacked training for making informed input into budgetary decisions. Lack of time and interest in budgetary matters was mentioned as a problem in another school. Several teachers noted that more than half of the staff in their school did not know or care who was on the budgetary committee. The principal of one middle school reportedly had to train her faculty and department heads in budgeting since they were not familiar with it.

One school district handled the additional time demands associated with increased budgetary responsibilities of department heads by giving them an additional administrative period each day.

Other Budget-Related Concerns. A number of science and mathematics faculty, noting the special needs of science departments for "consumables," such as glassware, specimens, and costly, "high tech" equipment, were concerned that science departments would be hurt if site councils decided to equalize spending across departments. This is an argument for at least some central control over school budget allocations. However, in the schools we examined, we found no actual instances of science (or mathematics) departments losing funds because of site-council equalizations. In fact, by and large, the faculty reported few problems in obtaining desired science and mathematics supplies and equipment.

Science teachers in one school mentioned concerns about whether they could receive the substantial amount of funds needed for a planned complete revision of curriculum through the school-wide budget process. "It will involve a lot of pleading and begging" to get the extra equipment and supplies to implement those changes.

Personnel in one district noted that decentralized budgeting highlights inequities related to the age of school buildings since it costs more to run old buildings and to introduce new technologies in them. For example, older buildings have no room for computer labs.

Education budget cutbacks created problems and frustrations for schools with increased budgetary authority. Even though science and mathematics faculty and other school personnel had greater budgetary authority, they not only had less to spend but had to decide where to take cuts.

Tight budgets may also tempt schools or departments to spend money as early as possible to avoid the risk of losing it later in the year. The result often is less desirable spending decisions and no "cushion" for unforeseen needs arising later. Similarly, tight budgets can inhibit the inclination to "try something new." Dade County had a trial program where schools were given an allocation for utilities and a rebate for money they saved, but the program was discontinued when the district budget situation worsened. Two districts that were allowing schools to carry funds over to the next year stopped because of deteriorating conditions.

Budget cutbacks can lead to loss of momentum in carrying out planned purchases. In one high school where the science and mathematics departments were using their increased budget flexibility to purchase computers and other technological materials, budget cutbacks thwarted their efforts to increase purchases.

The mathematics department head in one high school viewed district-wide budgetary problems in a brighter light, however. He believed that SBM plays a positive role when budgetary situations worsen because it makes staff feel that everyone is "in it together," induces them to pull together for the school as a whole rather than defending their own "empires." However, it seems clear that school district and individual school leaders have not communicated effectively that decentralization/SBM enables schools to decide for themselves what to do about reduced budgets rather than having such decisions imposed on them.

Training and Technical Assistance for Budgeting. Several school districts provided annual training or assistance on budgeting issues to such staff as new principals, assistant principals, school bookkeepers, and department heads. Prince George's County, for example, developed a video presentation to explain budgeting procedures under SBM, and made district budget analysts available to help schools. The district also gave schools a monthly balance sheet.

Changes in Science and Mathematics Education. Many schools among the ones we studied made changes in science and mathematics education that they attributed to budget decentralization. While these schools might not have been able to make these changes without SBM, the faculty clearly believed that these changes occurred much faster and often with less effort that would otherwise have been possible.

❑ One middle school purchased a variety of technologies that changed patterns of communication with students as well as instructional content. Science teachers were able to use computer software, video microscopes, and a satellite dish to download NASA programs, such as those on robotics or geology, which they likened to "taking students on a field trip without having to pay for it." The mathematics department could purchase manipulatives more quickly.

The same school used budget flexibility to modify the physical plant to enhance science and mathematics education. The old "open classrooms" were closed off, which enabled instructors to use group learning techniques without unduly disturbing other classes. Electric outlets were added at students' tables in science and mathematics classrooms so the new computers and other electric technology could be conveniently plugged in where needed. (Previously, outlets were at exterior walls.) The mathematics department purchased flat desks after discovering that the new manipulatives were sliding around on the old slanted desks.

This school also allocated funds for professional development and in-service training to improve instruction. For example, the science department head was able to attend summer classes on cooperative learning and integration of science, mathematics, and technology education, and share the information he obtained with other faculty.

❑ A high school purchased microscopes for every biology lab and computers for six computer labs. Both mathematics and science departments reported increased use of computers as a result.

❑ One high school purchased a software package for teaching algebra and videos featuring problem solving and statistics gathering in algebra classes. Another high school purchased algebra software, manipulatives such as algebra tiles, and calculators.

❑ A middle school's school-based decisions on the use of district-allocated technology funds affected how some science and mathematics classes were taught. Some teachers changed their role from lecturer to facilitator/coordinator of student learning. Students worked at computers individually, then came back to their group and shared what they had learned, thus becoming more involved in their own learning.

❑ Science and mathematics teachers in one high school traded off textbook funds to purchase manipulatives and other supplies.

❑ One middle school used budgetary decentralization to hire substitutes so that 10 mathematics teachers could attend workshops on the use of calculators and manipulatives.

❑ A number of schools used budget authority to improve science and mathematics education by dealing with disciplinary issues that were a detriment to learning. For example, one school fenced off an area that was used as a shortcut by outsiders, thus increasing security and reducing interruptions.

❑ Some schools used budget flexibility to help deal with students having academic or behavioral problems. One school initiated an after-school tutorial program and arranged for bus transportation to enable students to stay after school. Students with mathematics problems were major users of this program. One middle school hired a full-time teacher to tutor students in mathematics. A junior high school created a program for ninth grade students at risk of dropping out of school because of academic and behavioral problems. "Regular" classes also benefited by the removal of the disruptive or lagging students.

RECOMMENDATIONS

District Level

✓ 1. Decentralize budgeting decisions not only to the school level, but to departments and teaching teams as well. Provide them with a basic budget for such items as supplies, equipment, professional development, and substitute teachers, and let them determine how to allocate funds in each category.

2. Allow and encourage individual schools to consider personnel tradeoffs when departures occur. Encourage principals and site councils to involve departments and teaching teams in making such decisions.

✓ 3. Allow schools to transfer funds among accounts throughout the school year rather than only at the beginning of the year, so that they have the flexibility to respond to changing needs and opportunities.

4. Allow schools to carry over unspent funds from one school year to the next, but limit the size of the carryover.

5. Modify school district management information systems to provide budget information at the departmental level to assist school staff in tracking their budget status.

6. Allow schools and departments to do more of their own purchasing, but impose limits, such as central approval for items costing over certain amounts or more than school district listed prices.

7. Encourage schools and departments to link their budget decisions to the school's improvement plan (or other long-term plans).

8. Provide training in budgeting and purchasing, with different sessions for different kinds of staff (such as the principal, department heads, site council personnel, faculty, and school clerical staff).

School Level

9. Principals and site councils should further decentralize budget decisions to departments and/or teaching teams to the extent feasible, providing them with basic budgets (as outlined in number 1 above) and letting them determine how to allocate funds in each category.

10. School staff should take full advantage of budget authorities decentralized to them (such as those described above). Principals should encourage department heads and teachers to use these authorities, and, if needed, provide training, or assistance, or refer staff to district-provided training.

11. When personnel tradeoffs are feasible due to teachers' departures, science and mathematics departments could use these opportunities to review their needs for subject matter coverage and to seek replacement teachers for other courses that students need more than traditional offerings. Or, student/teacher ratio limits permitting, the dollars might be used for tutoring or other innovative purposes.

CHAPTER 3

Extent of Decentralization of Personnel Decisions

One of the three primary decision-making areas decentralized under SBM is personnel. (Budgeting, discussed in chapter 2, and curriculum/instructional decisions, discussed primarily in chapter 13, are the other two.) Traditional personnel decisions include hiring, firing, and staff assignments, such as selection of personnel for leadership positions (e.g., department heads, lead teachers).

FINDINGS

The extent of decentralization of personnel-related decisions to the school level varied considerably *among* the school districts we contacted, as did the extent to which these decisions were shared *within* the schools. Most commonly delegated to the school level were hiring and staff assignment, although staff assignments had traditionally been decentralized to the school level in most districts even before SBM or other recent decentralization efforts.

Decentralization of Hiring Decisions

Hiring decisions were delegated to the school level to some extent in virtually all districts we contacted, but generally to a limited degree. Mandatory limits on pupil/teacher ratios (imposed by the district or the state) and requirements for specific types of teachers—such as special education teachers—limited flexibility in hiring or assignment of teaching staff. Thus, decentralization related to hiring usually meant greater school input into *who* was to be hired for specific positions rather than the overall composition of the school staff.

The SBM schools we contacted thus generally participated in selecting new science and mathematics teachers but did not have sole authority over the process. The activities most commonly delegated to the school level were identifying preferred candidates from a district-supplied list of eligible candidates, interviewing candidates, and recommending hires to the school district. In at least some districts this kind of decentralization pre-dated SBM efforts. Only one district we contacted, Fort Worth, Texas, encouraged principals to recruit staff directly.

In a few school districts, schools were given a role in hiring principals and assistant principals, as well as teachers. School-level hiring authority sometimes even was extended to non-faculty, such as maintenance staff, paraprofessionals, or general office aides.

Most principals consulted other staff members in making hiring decisions. In some schools, the department head and at least some faculty members of the department concerned were involved in the hiring process. In others, the site council, or representatives from it, was used as a "search committee." In schools organized into teaching teams, faculty on the team being staffed usually participated in interviewing job candidates and making hiring recommendations.

Despite the faculty participation in hiring new teachers, principals generally made the final recommendation to the district. This was a sore spot in at least one school visited. In others, principals acknowledged that they could "veto" faculty recommendations, but never, or rarely, did so. One principal noted he had once "pushed" a teaching team to select a particular candidate to meet a need for a Hispanic role model on that team.

The procedures used to select principals were usually similar to those for hiring faculty. That is, the district advertised and screened candidates, selected faculty interviewed them, and the school made its recommendation to the district. In this case, however, faculty members involved in the process were primarily site council members. One approach was to use some or all site council members as the search committee. In one high school, a few site council members served as advisors to the central administration when a principal or assistant principal was being hired.

Although schools generally could not fire teachers, decentralization of staffing and budgeting authority enabled some schools to choose *how* to fill open faculty positions (i.e., to make hiring decisions). They could, for example, decide to replace departing faculty with teachers of different subjects, or use the salary allocated for the open position for non-faculty purposes.

Such hiring decisions occurred in a few schools, generally where the departing faculty member taught elective classes. In one middle school, the principal unilaterally decided to strengthen the school's science teaching capabilities by replacing an English teacher position with a science teacher who was also qualified to teach English. One high school "replaced" a guidance counselor position with summer workshop days for teachers.

■ *LIMITATIONS AND PROBLEMS*

There were two major limitations on the school role in hiring faculty, both related to employment contracts. First, only the districts had the legal authority to execute employment contracts with teachers; schools technically acted only in an advisory capacity with respect to hiring decisions. Second, in some districts, schools were encouraged (or sometimes obliged) to hire "surplus" teachers already under contract with the district before new teachers could be hired.

Similar limitations applied to the hiring of school administrators. One district temporarily suspended its policy of decentralizing principal-hiring authority for two schools because two individuals already under contract as principals had to be placed in those schools. District administrators saw this as a temporary measure, to apply only for the remaining year on their contracts, and intended to let the schools participate in hiring permanent principals subsequently.

It does not appear likely that contract restrictions can be eliminated. As one district administrator pointed out, "You can't hire good teachers without providing some kind of security in an employment contract." In giving autonomy to schools, the district may not violate property rights of individuals (as provided in contractual agreements).

Science and mathematics teachers and administrators we interviewed raised a variety of concerns related to decentralization of hiring decisions. A common theme was the degree to which hiring decisions were truly decentralized and/or shared among faculty. Issues raised focused on:

❑ The perception that faculty was not involved enough in hiring decisions, or that principals had too much authority or veto power over faculty.

❑ Concerns that the school district was not following the hiring recommendation made by the school. The decision of one district to reject a high school recommendation for a new principal left hard feelings among teachers in that school. One teacher noted, "These things make teachers cynical."

❑ Involvement of insufficient faculty in the hiring process (or the participation of only site council members).

Some other negative aspects of decentralizing faculty hiring decisions were reported. One district personnel administrator pointed out that shared decision making delays the hiring process: the more people involved at the school level, the longer to schedule and conduct candidate interviews. In addition, search committees need time to meet and reach a decision on candidates. In the worse case, the most desirable candidates may be hired away by another school during these procedural delays.

Another problem mentioned was the frequent need for staff hiring decisions during the summer. Since teachers were not always available to participate in the hiring process during the summer, the hiring choice was, by default, left to the principal and/or the district, defeating the intent of decentralization.

Decentralization of Firing Decisions

We did not find any case where schools were delegated authority to fire staff, primarily because teacher contracts and union agreements are made with the district, not the school. For example, if a school decided to "fire" a teacher who had a contract with the school district, the district would then have to find another position for that teacher. Seniority rules also come into effect in such situations, generally meaning that junior staff in some schools could be replaced by more senior staff "fired" by other schools.

In cutback situations, districts did delegate "firing" authority to schools, but only to meet a district-mandated number of *positions* or dollars that had to be cut. The Albuquerque district, which was undergoing budget cuts at the time of our visit, allowed schools to make termination decisions because of this situation. Each school was required to identify how it would achieve a 1.5 percent budget cut for the coming school year, including reductions in any type of staff. In another district, the high school we visited had been mandated to cut three faculty positions, and was given authority to decide where the cuts would be made. As might be expected, many teachers felt quite uncomfortable about making decisions to fire other teachers.

Decentralization of Staff Assignment Decisions

Some schools participated more in various kinds of staff assignment issues as a result of SBM or other decentralization efforts in their district. These activities included:

❏ Selecting leadership positions in their school, such as administrators, department heads, and leaders of teaching teams.

❏ Assigning teachers to regular positions and teaching teams.

❏ Trading off teaching lessons on certain subjects.

❏ Creating special-purpose positions, such as for special tutorial or disciplinary activities.

Science and mathematics faculty had a greater role in selecting staff for leadership positions in a few places as a result of SBM. Department heads in one high school were elected by faculty instead of appointed by principals, and in a district with district-wide SBM, each school decided on its own process for selecting department heads. However, the principal of one of these schools said that school-based leader selection was a mistake—people who were good at getting elected did not necessarily make good leaders. Some schools held elections for department chairs. In one high school, the principal decided that the principal and assistant principal would select department heads, but would invite teachers to apply for the positions.

Teachers could influence the process by encouraging specific teachers to apply.

In some middle schools organized into teaching teams, team members were given authority to choose their team leader.

A different kind of "leadership" role in Salt Lake City was related to its career ladder system. The career ladder established two "higher" levels of teacher classification: teacher leaders and teacher specialists. These job titles involved higher wages and additional responsibilities and were available to only a limited number of teachers in each school. Although the career ladder was instituted statewide, site councils were involved in selecting teachers for the higher positions.

In a small number of schools we contacted, decentralization enabled schools to create new leadership positions. For example, one middle school created a "leadership opportunity assistant principal," a new teacher leadership slot responsible for a range of administrative activities. A high school in the same district created a new assistant-to-the-principal position, which was filled by teachers interning for administrative positions.

Another kind of staff assignment decision decentralized within some schools was assignment of teachers to teaching teams. In two middle schools, for example, assignment to teams was based on a combination of teaching competencies needed by the team and the preference of the individual teachers and team members.

In one middle school we contacted, teachers within a specific department were able to make short-term reassignment decisions within or between teams through a "float" concept. Teachers could trade off teaching lessons, allowing them to take advantage of each other's particular competencies or strengths, or to help a particular class with a different teaching approach.

Another way schools used decentralized staffing capabilities was to create special-purpose positions to address needs specific to their schools and students. One middle school we contacted used budget and staffing flexibility to create a new after-school and summer tutorial program for at-risk students.

School funds were used to compensate teachers and aides for extra time spent on operating the program. A similar approach was used to provide teaching staff to supervise a program for students with disciplinary problems—a program that was initiated by teachers. Another middle school used staffing flexibility to assign one administrator to each grade level to supervise student discipline.

RECOMMENDATIONS

District Level

1. Encourage principals to involve department heads and faculty of the department(s) affected in the hiring process, such as in the interview process.

2. Encourage broad participation by school personnel in hiring principals and assistant principals, such as in the interview process.

3. Encourage principals to use sparingly their authority to overrule faculty hiring recommendations. Similarly, districts should use sparingly their authority to overrule the hiring preferences of the school for faculty members or school administrators. Principals or districts that overrule recommendations should inform the faculty or school and indicate their reasons.

4. Communicate clearly to faculty (and others) the legal restrictions on hiring and firing decisions. Principals and district administrators who are delegating hiring authority should identify ahead of time key constraints on hiring (e.g., that a particular school must fill a position with a certain type of skill or background).

5. Require schools to develop guidelines (within federal and state restrictions) on handling hiring decisions, including who will be involved in the process. (For example, in Santa Fe, the school district requires each school to develop an approved personnel selection plan covering such processes as selecting search committee members, interviewing procedures, and selecting the recommended candidate.) Alternatively, the district could provide hiring guidelines (but not mandates) to the schools.

6. Enable schools to redefine any vacancies to be filled (e.g., to seek a science teacher with strength in chemistry rather than biology), thus increasing school authority over faculty composition. Require that these decisions be based on a systematic school-needs assessment effort.

7. Develop a procedure whereby schools can seek waivers to rules and laws restricting flexibility over faculty composition (such as pupil/teacher ratios, requirements for specialized teachers, etc.). Such procedures would not guarantee that all waivers would be granted, but would give schools the opportunity to make a case for doing something different.

8. Give schools authority to substitute positions (i.e., to hire teachers with specialties more appropriate for that school's needs) or to use funds to interchange full-time, part-time, and paraprofessional positions within overall district guidelines (e.g., maximum student/teacher ratios for various types of classes). Since some of the decisions may involve switching teachers among departments, the affected departments in each school should participate in the decisions.

9. Give administrators of individual schools significant say in removal of problem staff from the school. However, the rights of the "problem" staff need also to be protected under teacher agreements and district procedures.

10. Work with the teachers' associations in each district to develop flexible contractual arrangements that will promote greater decentralization of staffing authority to the school level.

School Level

11. Principals and site councils should involve department heads and faculty of department(s) affected by hiring decisions in the hiring process, from interviewing through selecting preferred candidates, and in decisions to redefine vacant positions or make substitutions in positions.

12. Principals should make efforts to involve faculty in hiring decisions that need to be made during the summer months. For example, before the school year ends, seek volunteers or nominations for a summertime search committee whose members can make themselves available to assist in unexpected hiring decisions. Consider setting aside some funds to pay teachers a small "honorarium" for serving on search committees during the summer.

13. Principals should limit use of their "veto" authority over faculty hiring recommendations, and should inform faculty of their reasons for using it when they do.

14. Principals should inform faculty of legal restrictions or other constraints on hiring decisions in advance.

15. Where feasible and to the extent appropriate under state, district, and teacher association requirements, principals should involve faculty in making decisions regarding leadership positions within the school, assignments to teaching teams, short-term tradeoffs of teaching responsibilities to accommodate student or faculty needs, and special positions to meet special circumstances and school needs.

16. Principals and site councils should provide opportunities for departments and teaching teams to be involved in decisions regarding removal of problem staff from their department or team.

CHAPTER 4

School Site Councils

One of the features that distinguishes SBM from most other forms of decentralization is its use of a school-level (site-based) decision-making body, a "site council." (For convenience we will use the term "site council" or "council" in this report regardless of the names used in the respective schools or districts.) The function of the councils is to make decisions, or provide recommendations to the school administration (i.e., the principal) on issues of school-wide concern. These responsibilities can affect science and mathematics education since, for example, council decisions might impact department budgets, class schedules, staff availability, and so on.

FINDINGS

Site Council Duties and Responsibilities

Most often, site councils examined issues and recommended actions to the principal. Even if the district gave them "authority" to decide, the principal usually retained veto power. The faculty's faith in and support for the SBM system were undermined if they perceived that the principal vetoed their decisions too often, or vetoed major issues.

In virtually all schools, budgetary decisions were delegated to site councils—for example, developing the school budget, transferring monies among different line items during the year, or deciding how to spend specific discretionary accounts. Site councils typically did not have authority over hiring decisions, which were generally decentralized to the department hiring the new faculty member. In a few school districts, however, site councils participated in selecting new principals or assistant principals. Similarly, site councils were not generally responsible for curricular or instructional decision making, unless such matters arose in conjunction with other council responsibilities, such as in the development of school improvement plans. Curriculum and instructional matters were more commonly dealt with at the department or teaching team levels, or by special committees. (For a more detailed discussion of decentralized responsibilities under SBM, see chapters 2, 3, and 5.)

In some instances, science and mathematics faculties felt that the council was only a nominal player in decisions or was manipulated by the principal. Much of this perception appeared to be related to the principal's personality and/or the principal's willingness to override or ignore council recommendations. A few principals pointed out that they never, or very rarely, used their ability to veto to avoid violating the spirit of decentralized decision making.

The science and mathematics teachers we interviewed most often identified the following site council problems:

❑ Confusion about exactly what authority was delegated, and to whom.

❑ Perception that insufficient authority was delegated to the school level.

❑ Perception that authority was not sufficiently delegated *within* the school (i.e., that the principal did not adequately share decision-making authority with others in the school, such as the site council, departments, or teachers).

The problems arise because of a conflict between the recommended role of councils and the prescribed role of principals. Although the literature on SBM and much of the explanatory and "how to" material suggest that councils should be decision-making bodies—justifiably raising certain expectations for council members and other teachers—at the same time, districts hold principals accountable for what happens in their schools. Accordingly, principals will have full authority to override council decisions—either by formally vetoing them within the council, or by informally ignoring the decisions outside the council.

In addition to this sore spot, many teachers we interviewed were unclear about the council's extent of authority. In some districts, the schools themselves defined the scope of the council, in whole or in part, leading to variation in council responsibilities between schools within the same district. In others, councils were free to deal with any issue brought before them. While such arrangements may be consistent with the goal of decentralizing authority to the schools, they may also contribute to confusion about the extent of authority delegated to various participants.

Too much latitude—or lack of specificity—in what the council may address may result in poor use of council time. Two principals we interviewed expressed concern that their councils dealt with too many "trivial" issues that did not really need to be addressed at the school-wide level, such as establishing a school rule regarding gum-chewing in class.

On the other hand, site councils in several schools contacted had the major responsibility of developing or ratifying school plans (typically, School Improvement Plans) or related items such as mission statements or goals. Such documents were sometimes required as part of a school's proposal to participate in a district's SBM effort.

A council role in developing school improvement plans has the potential to be particularly important for improving education in science and mathematics (or other subjects). In some cases, schools initiated substantial changes through their School Improvement Plans. For example, some middle schools we contacted that adopted the "Re:Learning schools" model or similar approaches (e.g., using teams of teachers, more problem solving, and an interdisciplinary curriculum) included these changes in their School Improvement Plans. However, School Improvement Plans generally were not used to guide council—or administrative—decision making on an ongoing basis in the schools we examined.

Other important, but less widespread, responsibilities of site councils included seeking grants; approving grant proposals prepared by other school faculty or administrators; preparing requests for waivers of district, state, or union regulations; preparing requests for delegation of authority to the school level and/or drawing up procedures for SBM at the school level; and ratifying the school improvement plan (in cases where it was not developed by the council).

Composition of Site Council and Selection of Members

Site council composition is an important issue because of the council's role in decision making. In some districts, the school district specifies the composition of the council wholly or partly. For example, site councils at SBM schools in Hillsborough had to include the principal, assistant principal, one teachers' association representative, and one non-faculty staff member, with the remainder determined by the schools. Some districts imposed other parameters on council composition. For example, Albuquerque required 50 percent of council members to be teachers. In over half the schools, the principal or an assistant principal were formal members of the site council.

Science and mathematics teachers or department heads were members of the site council in many of the schools we contacted. In many, if not most, schools contacted, the district or school required representation from each department or curricular area on the council.

In one high school which had dropped required department representation to control the size of the council, the head of the department expressed concern that the teachers elected at large might be too chauvinistic toward their own departments. (However, this concern was not shared by the science department head or faculty at the same school, whose department was similarly not represented.)

Some schools chose to consider all faculty members as members of the site council, although this approach was not common. In one such school, only a small group of 8 to 10 teachers regularly participated in council meetings, despite the view that all faculty were council members.

Schools contacted used various methods of selecting particular council members. Some districts specified how some or all council members were to be selected, while others left it to the schools to decide on the process. For example, Albuquerque stipulated that representatives of teachers and other unionized school staff (such as educational assistants and secretaries) were to be elected by their peers.

In some cases, stipulations about council makeup—whether defined by the district or by the school itself—had the effect of self-selecting some or all members. For example, in a middle school in Prince George's County, where department chairs and instructional team leaders were stipulated for the faculty component of the council, the individuals holding these positions automatically became council members.

Most commonly, council members were elected by their constituencies, generally departments or teaching teams. A few schools held at-large elections. In a smaller number of cases, council members volunteered to serve.

In addition to faculty representation, site councils frequently included one or more parents or other community representatives. For example, a middle school in Fort Worth included three parents (elected by the PTA) and one community member as part of the school's management team. The parents and community members were non-voting members.

The Adams County Twelve Five Star school district (Northglen, Colorado) included parents, students, and community representatives on its school improvement team (site council), with parents in the majority. All had the same voting rights as the other members of the team.

Student representation on councils was an option left to the schools in most districts. In one district, student representation was required at the high school level. In another, councils were required to be representative of all school constituencies, including students.

Some faculty members felt that the students, parents, or community representatives on the site council did not have sufficient knowledge about internal school operations to provide meaningful input. However, the science and mathematics teachers and school administrators we contacted did not identify any specific instances of problems related to student or parent representatives on the site council.

Salt Lake City schools handled this concern by creating a separate School Community Council (SCC) consisting of community representatives, in addition to a site council composed of school staff. The SCC dealt with issues related to school policy and those of particular interest to the community, such as school boundaries, while the site council addressed any issue related to day-to-day operation of the school. In a few cases, the SCC took part in evaluating the school's principal. The district was deliberating about unifying the two types of councils into one body.

In some districts, parents or community representatives were included as non-voting members school site councils. A similar approach was used in some cases with other affected groups, such as union members. For example, schools in Hillsborough County were required to have an advisory committee consisting of union members in addition to their site councils. The advisory committee provided input on budget and goal setting.

Voting Procedures Used by Site Councils

Voting procedures were an issue with school personnel only in cases where the procedures were unclear or perceived to be unfair. However, different voting rules or practices could also result in different outcomes or decisions.

The concept of "consensus" decision making was common, both in the SBM literature and among the schools we contacted. A number of schools we visited used what they called "consensus" decision making on the site council. Some schools used "regular" voting (defined variously) in cases where consensus could not be reached.

However, we found uncertainty about what "consensus" meant and how it was to be achieved in practice. A number of the science and mathematics teachers and administrators we contacted were unsure of what consensus meant in operational terms. For example, did it mean that everyone on the council (100%) approved of ("voted for") a decision, or that a majority favored it? If the latter, was a simple majority sufficient, or was some specific decision rule (e.g., two-thirds majority) required? Alternatively, did consensus mean that everyone had an opportunity to give their views, and that all agreed to support a specific decision? The latter definition of consensus was included in the union contract language establishing Albuquerque's SBM effort.

Voting rules were not always spelled out in council by-laws or other documents related to SBM procedures. For example, in a Santa Fe high school, council by-laws identified two-thirds vote as the consensus, and required a quorum of 51 percent of the council members.

Several schools altered the decision rule, and even the forum for voting, according to the nature, or importance of, the issue in question. Some brought particularly important issues to full faculty meetings for discussion and/or voting, rather than to the site council, or suggested that this practice be adopted. Examples of such topics included policies, such as a new school-wide attendance policy; major modifications in educational approach, such as becoming an "essential" or "Re:Learning school;" and budgetary or spending matters. Similarly, some schools delayed decisions on particularly important or controversial issues so that each department could provide input to site council members. One school, which typically made decisions in full faculty meetings, varied the "decision rule" according to the importance of the issue. For example, it used a simple majority vote to determine whether to change the school schedule, but it required a two-thirds majority vote to select which of several proposed schedules to adopt. The faculty was consulted about which decision rule it wanted to use for specific issues. (In general, however, the school tried to work by consensus rather than voting.)

Special Science and Mathematics Concerns

Although some science and mathematics faculty expressed fear that site councils would not allocate needed funds for science and mathematics equipment and supplies when reviewing budgets, we found, surprisingly, that the special funding needs of these departments were seldom voted down by their site councils. At least in the schools we examined, the science and mathematics departments did quite well in justifying and securing their perceived needed funding, even though their departments received substantially larger amounts than others.

RECOMMENDATIONS

District Level

1. Clearly specify the authority and role of the site council. The school principal should be asked, in turn, to make that clear to school staff. In the early stages, the district and school may not, themselves, be clear as to what the council's role should be. Even then, the administration should, at least, indicate the gray zones that exist.

2. Urge principals to take considerable care in exercising their veto power over site council decisions. Frequent vetoes, especially on major recommendations, will undermine faculty confidence in the site council process.

School Level

3. Principals should give the site councils an important role in developing School Improvement Plans or similar strategic/long-range school planning activities. They should also advise the council to seek and encourage input from the full staff.

4. Site council guidelines should specify that all departments should be represented on the council, probably by someone elected by that department's faculty. To alleviate teachers' perceptions (and irritation) that they are not adequately represented on the council and do not have adequate opportunity to provide real input into the council's deliberations, schools should select council members by some form of "democratic process."

5. Principals and site council members should clarify council voting procedures and the definition of such ambiguities as "consensus." Consider multiple voting rules, based on the

importance of the issue. Clearly communicate the decision rules in use both to council members and to the faculty in general. Rules should be spelled out in council by-laws and in any other documents describing SBM procedures and operations.

6. Site councils should consider ways of obtaining input from the entire faculty, such as holding a full-faculty vote on issues of particular importance. More inclusive deliberations can soothe feelings of non-council members and reduce complaints about the representativeness of council members, decision rules used, etc. A mechanism shall be developed by which council members can obtain input from other faculty members, especially those in their departments, on issues facing the council.

7. Principals and site councils should obtain input from affected departments or faculty, such as science and mathematics, on decisions with implications for particular subject areas.

CHAPTER 5

Role of Science and Mathematics Department Heads

An issue usually not raised in SBM and decentralization is their effect on science and mathematics department heads. For example: How does decentralization affect the traditional authorities of department heads? And do, or should, department heads have a special role to play in relation to SBM?

FINDINGS

In most schools we contacted, SBM did not appear to make much difference in the role of science and mathematics department heads within the school. In a few cases, however, it appeared to have strong effects, leading in some instances to an increased role, but in others a decreased role.

Increased Roles

The role of science and mathematics department heads increased in one school because all department heads were automatically included on the site council. In some other schools, science and mathematics heads served on the council but their inclusion was not mandated. Including department heads on the council helped ensure that their position was not diminished by the introduction of the new school decision-making body. In addition, their increased responsibilities to solicit and represent their faculty's views on decision-making bodies were seen as an expansion of their role in some schools.

Some science and mathematics department heads reported that their inclusion on site councils or other decision-making bodies led to involvement in new activities, such as developing School Improvement Plans and making school-level budgeting decisions. Some heads also received more school-level data as site council members than as department heads, increasing their awareness of other school issues. In effect, their role expanded in concert with their increased levels of participation and information.

In a few cases, schools acting under decentralization created a separate decision-making body for department heads, thus increasing their role within the school. This occurred in schools both with and without site councils. For example:

❑ A Poway high school established a committee composed of department heads, guidance counselors, the principal, and the assistant principal, which met monthly to address a wide range of policy issues. The school also had a site council. Departments also held their own meetings twice a month to discuss major issues, which were then brought to the committee.

❑ A Kalispell, Montana, high school established two decision-making bodies: a committee of department chairs (which also included the principal and assistant principals) and "department teams" for each subject area, consisting of the department chair and all teachers in the department. The department chair committee was the primary decision-making body in the school. The teams met twice a month, which reportedly fostered good, cooperative relations within departments. Issues raised by department teams were brought up at the monthly department chair committee meetings for disposition.

❑ A Prince William County middle school created a committee of department heads and school administration personnel in addition to its advisory council (site council). The department head committee appeared to have a stronger role than the advisory council, since it was involved in formulating the budget and the school plan.

Other aspects of decentralization—such as greater sharing of hiring and budgetary decision making—also increased the role of department heads in a small number of cases. The mathematics department head of one middle school noted that decentralization had given him greater involvement in interviewing and hiring new teachers than he had ever had before. In one high school, the mathematics department head reported that before SBM, department heads had participated in hiring, but that after SBM, they had the final responsibility, as well as the responsibility for including other teachers, in the selection process.

In one high school, department heads reported a considerable increase in their role because of greater delegation of budgeting responsibility. In this school, the size of the budget controlled at the department level increased as a result of SBM; departments were given responsibility over funds for supplies, equipment, equipment maintenance, and professional development, and could hire part-time teachers and pay teachers to teach an extra period. As a result, the amount of ordering at the department level increased substantially, and department heads were allocated an extra period for dealing with budgetary and other SBM matters. Department heads believed that their increased control over the budget enhanced their ability to bring about changes in their faculty. They also felt they played an important role in the success of overall delegation of authority associated with SBM in that school.

Decreased Roles

Assignment of various school-level responsibilities to site councils or similar bodies decreased the role or importance of some science and mathematics department heads, particularly when some council responsibilities had formerly been assigned to departments. This effect of SBM was recognized in a particularly dramatic way in one Colorado high school:

❏ Soon after SBM was implemented, department head positions were eliminated and their responsibilities were distributed among the teachers within each department. Responsibilities were assigned for a two-year period and rotated among department members to enable everyone to be involved. Faculty decided on this approach because most major decisions affecting departments were delegated to various committees (such as the budget and curriculum committees) created in response to SBM.

The additional compensation and release time formerly provided to department heads was reallocated for other purposes, including teacher release time for such activities as grant development and curriculum development and coordination, and for substitutes to enable teachers to attend workshops, seminars, etc.

The change that appeared to have the greatest effect in diminishing the role of department heads and departments in the schools we contacted was adoption of *teaching teams*, especially at middle schools. While teaching teams are not necessarily associated with SBM, they are an important form of decentralization and, thus, are of relevance here. Science and mathematics teachers in those settings generally reported that they interacted primarily with other teachers on their team rather than with teachers in their own department or with their department heads. Joint planning times were typically scheduled for teaching team members, but little or no time was set aside for "regular" department meetings in these schools. In addition, principals began interacting more with teaching teams and their team leaders than with department heads as the teams became the focal point for instructional efforts. The mathematics department head in one middle school reported that he felt he had become a chair in name only because of the team structure the school adopted. Although he felt that departments should meet at least quarterly to address curriculum issues, testing, and district requirements, he was reluctant to call meetings that frequently because faculty were so busy with team-related issues. He speculated as to whether departments were necessary in the team context, and thought their role should be reevaluated.

This evolution of responsibilities away from department heads to teaching teams did not appear to have caused major problems. By and large, the science and mathematics faculties believed the resulting arrangements were an improvement overall. Some faculty noted that the role of the department head was still necessary in middle schools, even with teaching teams to maintain integration and coordination *between* grades.

RECOMMENDATIONS

District Level

1. Leave decisions about changes in the role of department heads under SBM up to the schools, specifically, department heads, faculty, and the principal.

School Level

2. Principals should arrange to provide department heads (and perhaps leaders of teaching teams) with special training and technical assistance to cover added responsibilities for such functions as budgeting, procurement, and personnel. The role of science and mathematics department heads likely will be increased under SBM because of their added responsibility in budgeting, procurement, and personnel matters (except where teaching teams are used).

3. Principals and site councils should avoid inadvertently diminishing the role of department heads by delegating their responsibilities to site councils. Principals should involve department heads—or solicit their input—in major school decisions, such as school budgets and school improvement plans, along with the site council. Alternatively, SBM guidelines or procedures should reserve some decision-making authority to department heads and administrators.

4. School administrators and staff should proactively reevaluate and redefine the role of department heads when introducing teaching teams.

CHAPTER 6

Involvement of Parents and Students

Probably the primary way in which parents and students have been brought into SBM activities is by participation on school site councils and other committees such as "school improvement teams." In such instances, usually only a very small number of parents or students are involved. The question arises as to whether this involvement has a significant impact on school activities and, thus, ultimately on science and mathematics education.

Parents' at-home support of their children's learning activities is almost universally accepted as being an important, and probably critical, role in the education of their children. This support entails providing both an atmosphere conducive to learning and direct help to their children in their school work. While this involvement is not usually an explicit component of SBM, it is an important element that SBM can potentially enhance.

FINDINGS

Parent Involvement

Most of the school system personnel who we interviewed reported that parents continue to be uninvolved or under-involved in school operations or activities despite the presence of SBM programs or policies.

Some schools structured school site councils or other committees such as "school improvement teams" to include parents as members. Other school systems adopted policies that encouraged the participation of parents in classroom, instructional, or administrative activities.

■ *PARENTS PARTICIPATION IN DECISION-MAKING BODIES*

Less than half the schools we examined reported parents directly involved in the decision-making process through membership on school governing bodies such as site councils and school management teams. Usually only one or two parents were council members. A few schools structured their governance councils to include more parents than teachers or other school personnel. In other schools/school districts, an equal number of parents, teachers, and others sat on the councils.

❑ An Adams County Twelve Five Star high school structured its school improvement team (one of the school's decision-making groups) to include more parents than teachers and other school representatives: 12 parents, 3 teachers, 2 administrators, 3 students, and 1 or 2 community representatives.

❑ A middle school in Fort Worth designed its site council (the school's primary SBM decision-making body) to include an equal number of parents and teachers. The parents who served on the council were elected by the PTA. Their input into council decisions was encouraged, and they were allowed to vote on issues.

❑ Salt Lake City designed the SBM decision-making structure in all its schools to include two decision-making bodies: a School Improvement Council (SIC), the primary decision-making group whose members were drawn from school staff (teachers, principal, etc.), and a School Community Council (SCC), which consisted of the SIC members plus parent representatives. The SCC played an advisory role and provided an information link to parents and the community. The responsibilities of the SCC were relatively limited, although it often had the responsibility of confirming decisions made by the SIC, and, in some schools, participated in the annual evaluation of principal performance.

By and large, the science and mathematics faculty members whom we interviewed did not perceive much substantial influence of the parents in their educational activities. This assessment could be accurate, or parent input might not be obvious as it filters through site council decision making. Faculty did not appear to be particularly concerned that parents were not very involved in decision making, although a few principals stated that they wanted greater parental involvement, and school staff generally supported the concept of greater parental involvement in schools.

■ *STRATEGIES TO INCREASE PARENTAL INVOLVEMENT*

Some schools adopted other measures to increase the involvement of parents in school activities, such as:

❑ A high school in the Hillsborough school district shifted its parent-teacher meetings from daytime to evenings (at the suggestion of teachers) to increase parent attendance. Parent attendance at PTA meetings doubled.

❑ A Dade County middle school surveyed parents (originally annually, but later every three years because of the cost) to obtain feedback on various school characteristics. The survey results were reported in the school's annual report and used to prepare the School Improvement Plan.

❑ The principal of an Albuquerque high school undertook several efforts to increase communication with parents. He frequently attended PTA meetings and provided updates on activities of the school's management council and other committees. He also held periodic meetings ("fireside chats") with the parents association to discuss and solicit feedback on important issues affecting the school, such as proposed changes in the number of credits needed for graduation. He also used his regular column in the school newspaper (sent to all parents) to report on council activities and other changes, and to encourage parents to attend meetings of the council and other school events.

❑ Middle schools in Albuquerque and Santa Fe, which were using the "Re:Learning" approach to teaching, invited parents to attend periodic presentations of student "portfolios" (examples of each student's best efforts in a variety of subject areas and formats). One school called this a "Celebration of Learning," and featured student performances as well as portfolios on display. In addition, one of these schools also set aside a couple of days early in the school year for faculty to meet with parents and children and to discuss plans and expectations for the year.

❑ An intermediate school in Salt Lake City undertook a particularly ambitious effort to increase communication with parents, parental involvement in their children's education, and student accountability. The site council decided to use its increased budgetary flexibility over the school's technology funds to establish "Parentlink," a computerized phone-link system. Each teacher entered a daily message into the system, including information about what was covered in class, homework assignments, upcoming exams, the next day's lessons, special activities, etc. Each class had a code number that parents could dial to get information about that class to keep abreast of assignments in cases of absence, or if the student was uncertain about homework assignments. The school planned to add a feature enabling teachers to enter test and course grades in the system so parents could be informed about their child's performance.

❑ A high school in Albuquerque was able to benefit from the scientific background of several parents. Three parents who were scientists in a nearby Department of Energy laboratory developed and offered to teach an advanced physics course at the school. These parents continued teaching the class even after their children had graduated, as part of a partnership arrangement between the school district and the laboratory.

❑ Albuquerque was able to provide training related to decentralization for parents by participating in a national organization's training and technical assistance program. This organization provided training workshops for parents (sponsored by existing parents' organizations) covering topics related to the district's restructuring efforts, such as creating a school vision and School Improvement Plan, and assessing a school's culture/climate. Although a number of school districts or schools offered training to parents in their capacities as members of site councils, the Albuquerque training was only for parents, not for all site council members.

A very few schools undertook innovative attempts to more directly involve parents of students having school problems.

❑ With the flexibility provided by SBM, a high school in Dade County introduced a school-within-a-school program as a drop-out prevention program for ninth-graders. As one element of the program, teachers sometimes visited homes of students who had substantial problems. Teachers reported usually getting good support from the parents (though attendance at the program's evening open house was poor).

❑ Science and mathematics teachers in several of the middle schools organized into teaching teams brought in parents of students having major problems so that all of the team's teachers could jointly discuss these problems with the parent. Teachers reported this approach was more effective than one teacher discussing the problem with the parent.

❑ The principal of a Hillsborough middle school was *considering* starting a new initiative to improve parenting skills and education, especially for their large number of single parents, an effort he could implement under SBM.

Student Involvement

We did not find a significant level of student involvement in decision making at the schools we examined. Student participation, when present, consisted primarily of representation on school governance bodies, such as site councils, school improvement teams, or advisory committees. Students were represented on school governance bodies in 4 of the 10 high schools examined.

❑ The school improvement team at a high school in the Adams County Twelve Five Star district location included three student representatives. The responsibilities of the school improvement team were somewhat limited and consisted primarily of establishing the school's improvement goals and developing the School Improvement Plan.

❑ Students at a Santa Fe high school were represented on the school's executive governing council. Student membership on the council was limited to one representative.

❑ A Poway high school included a larger number of students in the decision-making process. Students made up about one-third of the school's site council 13-person membership. The responsibilities of the site council were limited, consisting primarily of developing the school's annual improvement plan and monitoring the use of school improvement funds.

❑ Two school districts, Hillsborough and Prince William County, annually surveyed their students (as well as parents, teachers, and other school personnel) to obtain their feedback on school services.

One principal at a middle school and one at a high school felt that students should be more involved in decision making. However, they presented no specifics as to ways and means. Student input, even at the high school level, clearly was not a high priority, as evidenced by the few cases of student involvement and the few suggestions from school personnel on student involvement.

RECOMMENDATIONS

District Level

1. Encourage schools to include parent and student representation on site councils or similar bodies; expand their efforts to encourage participation of these groups in a variety of school endeavors; and seek input from parents and students.

2. Disseminate information and provide training to school administrators and faculty on effective ways to increase parental and student involvement.

School Level

3. Principals and site councils should increase parent participation on school site councils and other advisory bodies by

including parents on the school advisory bodies; creating linkages between the site council and the parents association; inviting parents to attend site council meetings; allowing parents to speak and present issues, concerns, and grievances at site council meetings when feasible; keeping parents, via the parents association, abreast of issues affecting the schools and decisions to be made; and disseminating copies of meeting minutes and/or agendas to the parents association for redistribution via the association's own communication media.

4. Principals and site councils should regularly, perhaps annually, survey parents and students to obtain their views on the school and its performance, including that of individual departments, and to ask their opinions on improvements that the school can make. Feed the resulting information back to school staff and individual departments. The survey need not focus only on issues directly related to SBM, but may touch on other important school characteristics (such as safety, physical condition of equipment and facilities, etc.).

3. Faculty should give greater attention to developing innovative ways to encourage and help parents of students with substantial problems. While this may add extra work for school staff, it is likely to pay off in less classroom stress and more educational progress. Parents may particularly need help relating to science and mathematics subjects (such as that provided by the University of California's Family Mathematics Program).

6. Science and mathematics departments should periodically seek student input into ways that science and mathematics can be made more interesting and attractive. Meetings with substantial numbers of students could be held periodically to identify desirable improvements both in the curriculum and in extracurricular science and mathematics activities. Students may well be an untapped source of innovative ideas for science and mathematics departments, which should be encouraged in a SBM/decentralized environment.

CHAPTER 7

Ongoing Communication within the School Building

After implementing its version of SBM, a school will need to implement information exchange relevant to SBM-generated activities. Two new kinds of communication are indicated:

❏ Communication about SBM decisions and issues from decision-making bodies or the school administration *to faculty* and, where appropriate or relevant, to other parties (such as other school staff, students, and parents).

❏ Input *from faculty* to decision-making bodies and/or the school administration.

Both these kinds of communication are of particular concern under SBM. The SBM process at most schools generally is structured so that a relatively small group of individuals (typically the site council) is directly involved in across-department decisions. However, there is also a need to communicate with other faculty and school staff. Inadequate communication is just as detrimental to SBM efforts as lack of information.

FINDINGS

Inadequate communication between the site council and faculty was a problem commonly mentioned by science and mathematics teachers at the schools we examined, even in schools that used one or more of the communication mechanisms described below. Because of insufficient information, teachers who were not on the site council often felt that SBM did not make a difference or that nothing was happening. Without mechanisms to allow teachers to have input into the SBM process, they felt left out and frustrated with SBM. Such feelings promoted general dissatisfaction with, or lack of interest in, SBM, and eroded faculty support.

Most schools used a combination of approaches to communicate about SBM. Most commonly, council members disseminated information by word-of-mouth and acted as a conduit for input from other faculty (much as an elected representative to any governing body). Another common mechanism for sharing information was the distribution of council meeting minutes.

Neither mechanism was completely satisfactory. While site council members were generally considered to be responsible for reporting to their "constituencies" and for conveying the views of these constituencies to the council, this approach had some serious drawbacks, which may be why many schools did not rely on this method alone. Three problems were common:

❏ The site councils did not include representatives of each department or other relevant groups (such as teaching teams). To remedy an apparent communications problem, one middle school in Salt Lake City modified site council membership to ensure that one teacher from each of the three teachers' lunch periods was included. The principal believed that informal communication among teachers during their lunch periods would be a more effective means of communication than the formal method.

❑ Council representatives did not have a regular forum for reporting back to and getting input from their constituencies. In particular, we found few regular arrangements for representatives to routinely obtain substantial input on issues *from* their constituencies. Department meetings were infrequent, for example, or so brief or taken up with departmental-level discussions, that there was little time for discussing SBM issues except in a cursory way.

❑ The representatives, even where they had such a forum, did not consistently *use* the forum to report on SBM issues or to obtain input.

We found the second approach, distribution of council minutes, or similar summaries of council meetings, implemented in a variety of ways.

❑ Minutes or summaries of site council meetings were commonly distributed to all faculty and staff among the schools we contacted. They were typically placed in staff mailboxes within a few days of council meetings. However, some of the teachers in these schools still felt there was not enough communication about SBM activities in their school.

❑ Simply posting minutes, or leaving a stack of them in a central location for teachers to pick up (the practice in a small number of schools), was even less likely to keep teachers informed than directly distributing them.

❑ Two schools used the school newspaper to provide SBM-related information. One school regularly summarized council meeting minutes in its newspaper. In the other, major SBM-related "news" was occasionally covered in news stories or in the principal's regular column. Another school reported major decision items in the weekly staff newsletter.

❏ The principal in a Salt Lake City middle school tendered a standing invitation for faculty to join him for lunch after council meetings so that he could brief them on the meeting and answer their questions.

❏ One Hillsborough school set aside time one day each month for discussion of SBM committee issues in whole-school meetings following regular departmental meetings.

❏ A Kalispell high school established department teams for science and mathematics (as well as other departments), where each team consisted of the department chair and all the teachers in the department. A committee of department chairs was a primary decision-making body in the school. Teams met twice a month. The department chairs relayed issues raised by the teams to the school's monthly department chair meeting.

In contrast to site council meetings, school faculty did not see a need to circulate "minutes" or reports on decisions of *teaching teams* to all faculty members, since these teams primarily focused on matters related to their own teams and students. In one Albuquerque middle school we visited, teaching teams posted informal "minutes" or notes of meetings on the bulletin board in the faculty lounge to keep other teachers informed.

RECOMMENDATIONS

District Level

1. Emphasize the importance of in-school communication in training provided to school-level staff, and provide infor-

mation about communication measures such as those described below.

School Level

2. Site councils should include a representative of each department in the site council, where feasible.

3. Principals and site council officers should continually remind council members of their communication role. This should be part of the description of responsibilities for council members and should be emphasized to new members. Provide periodic reminders of this responsibility to all members through announcements at council or staff meetings, memos, etc.

4. Site council officers should send council members a copy of the minutes *promptly* after council meetings with a reminder that they should report on the meeting to their constituencies and obtain their input prior to future meetings.

5. Principals should ask department heads and teaching team leaders to set aside time during their regular meetings for council representatives to discuss SBM-related issues and obtain faculty input.

6. Principals and site council officers should use school newspapers, newsletters, and inside-school computerized networks as additional mechanisms for conveying information about SBM. These also can be forums for distributing information about decisions of individual teaching teams that affect, or may be of interest to, others.

7. Principals and site council officers should schedule informal, optional meetings—perhaps during teacher lunch periods—for staff briefings on council meetings or SBM-related

issues. Briefings might be presented by the principal, site council chair, or other council members.

8. Principals should reserve time for regular discussions relating to SBM between council members and faculty (perhaps associated with regularly scheduled meetings or events). For example, have someone provide a brief report on site council decisions and SBM issues at regular faculty meetings

9. Site councils should open their meetings to anyone who wishes to attend, and distribute meeting announcements and agendas well in advance to all staff. Principals and site council members should encourage faculty and others who are not council members to attend and participate.

10. Principals should hold special full-faculty meetings to discuss or vote on SBM or non-SBM topics of particular importance or interest, or add such items to regularly scheduled all-staff meetings.

11. Site council officers should distribute site council meeting agendas in advance (whether or not meetings are open) and let teachers submit items for inclusion on the agenda.

12. Principals and site council officers should encourage site council representatives to schedule meetings with other department faculty a few days prior to council meetings to solicit input on issues that the council expects to discuss and perhaps vote on at the meeting.

13. Principals and site council officers should develop other systematic mechanisms for teachers—or others—to facilitate faculty *input* to the council. For example:

   • Place a SBM suggestion box in the teacher's lounge or other central location.

   • Designate a column in the school newsletter or newspaper for publishing staff and student input to the council or administration (similar to a "letter to the editor" section).

If the school introduces a computerized network, staff could input comments directly through the network.

- When council agendas are distributed, include a return page on which teachers can comment on the agenda or provide other input. Establish a central drop-off point for these prior to the meeting.

- Set aside time at council meetings to report on and discuss the input obtained through these mechanisms.

14. Principals should encourage science and mathematics departments to cover in their meetings not only issues relating to SBM processes (such as issues being discussed by the site council and the department's own budget), but also innovation opportunities deriving from their enhanced roles (and the school flexibility), such as practices currently being tried in the department and ideas that should be considered for future trial.

15. Principals or site council officers should survey staff to determine if they are receiving adequate information about SBM-related matters, and have sufficient opportunity to provide input. The site council or the principal's office should periodically (perhaps annually) send a brief questionnaire to all faculty to assess, as part of their periodic evaluation of the SBM process, whether communication is adequate and to ask how to improve it.

CHAPTER **8**

Special SBM Training Needs at the School Level

W ithout adequate training, school staff who become significantly involved in decision making outside their traditional areas of responsibility (such as budgeting, procurement, and personnel), or are not accustomed to group decision making, can often feel frustrated, impatient, and generally unhappy about the process and its outcomes. As a result, the process may be poorly implemented, leading to wasted time.

FINDINGS

S BM-related training for school-level personnel—both start-up and ongoing—was a major and consistently raised concern of science and mathematics faculty and school administrators who we interviewed. Training was supported for all categories of school-level personnel, including teachers, school administrators (principals and vice principals), site council members, and classified (school counselors) and support/clerical personnel.

Most of the school systems we examined provided some SBM training to school-level personnel to facilitate and support the decentralization effort. They acknowledged that teachers, principals, and other school staff needed training to enable them to quickly and efficiently function as participants in decision making for their schools, and also to undertake the new responsibilities associated with SBM. District-level personnel needed training in new responsibilities, too.

School administrators and several teachers, including many of the science and mathematics teachers, associated the extent of training they received with the level of school district commitment to SBM.

Type of Training

■ START-UP TRAINING

All categories of school personnel (teachers, department heads, site council members) indicated that SBM training, particularly start-up training, is critical to the successful implementation of SBM programs. Many science and mathematics teachers who we interviewed reported a reluctance to participate in decision-making activities (such as joining site councils or committees), because they felt they lacked the knowledge and skills to perform efficiently as decision makers. One principal noted, "You can't expect teachers to be administrators without having had training in it."

Most school districts we examined provided some start-up or program initiation training to school-level personnel. This training was often funded centrally by the district and perhaps the state. District-funded training was usually conducted by consultants and consisted of orientations in basic SBM and shared-governance principles for school administrators and other members of the school staff. Other school districts provided start-up SBM training to principals or school administrators and relied on them to train teachers and other staff.

Most of the schools held an initial two- or three-day training session for teachers and school administrators; a few school districts conducted more intensive training, and a few did not provide any formal training at all. Training typically was presented as in-service workshops, seminars, or conferences, and consisted of an orientation in the following topics: a) how to develop and prepare school mission statements (statements of school improvement goals and objectives); b) shared governance principles/techniques; c) consensus building; d) team building; e) conflict resolution; and f) problem solving. Start-up training reflected individual differences in schools and their districts.

❑ The Santa Fe school district participated in an intensive two-day SBM training conference for teachers and school administrators offered by a local university in conjunction with a national foundation. The training session focused on collegiality, staff development, and consensus building issues and themes.

❑ Teachers at a Santa Fe middle school received SBM training combined with training in restructuring ("Re:Learning") principles, which the school was also adopting. The in-service sessions focused on cooperative learning and alternative instructional methods, as well as decision-making and role building skills. Some teachers were also sent to other schools to observe alternative decision-making and instructional methods practices.

❑ A Prince George's County high school provided a series of summer workshops on academic teaming and cooperative strategies and budgeting procedures. The workshops were funded by SBM funds allocated by the county. The county also offered a separate two-hour session on budgeting procedures to assist school staff in assuming budgeting responsibilities.

❏ Adams County Twelve Five Star school district provided a significant level of training to schools at the beginning of its SBM and school improvement implementation process. The approach was two-tiered: an educational consulting firm provided training to a selected group of school representatives (teachers, administrators, parents, and students) in school improvement/SBM processes, and the superintendent of schools, acting in the role of trainer, presented school improvement and SBM process orientations at all schools in the district. The superintendent of schools also developed a facilitator's guide to assist the district and schools in implementing SBM.

❏ In Salt Lake City, the Salt Lake Teachers Association and the Utah Education Association offered initial training on shared governance for site council members.

❏ In the Kalispell school district, the superintendent acted as the trainer for the district, visiting all seven district schools and conducting two- to three-hour sessions on shared decision making and collaborative management for principals and other school administrators. The school administrators in turn provided orientations to department heads and teachers, and department heads trained other teachers.

❏ In Poway, no formal training is supplied: each new administrator is paired with a mentor, and each department provides guidance as part of "the way we do business."

Few districts supplied initial training, or training-like experiences, for central-level personnel.

❏ In Salt Lake City, the district-wide committee established to introduce SBM received extensive training. This committee

met weekly over an eight-month period to observe and review information about SBM programs in 13 other states and
to develop a district SBM policy.

❑ A central administrator responsible for SBM in one district
called the initial lack of start-up training for central-level
personnel a "major oversight." In the absence of training in
the basic concepts of shared decision making, some central
staff were reluctant to relinquish decision-making authorities to the schools, impeding a smooth implementation of
SBM. This district began providing training to central personnel two or three years after SBM was introduced in the
district.

■ *ONGOING TRAINING*

The overwhelming majority of teachers and other school personnel endorsed some type of ongoing SBM training in addition to
start-up training. However, cutbacks in state funding for many
school systems affected their ability to provide such training.

Teachers in just under half the SBM schools we examined
receive some type of ongoing teacher training, normally as
in-service teacher training. SBM-related topics usually are combined with instructional or curricula reform practices. The amount
and degree of ongoing training provided to school staff varies
by district and by school within a district.

❑ Adams County Twelve Five Star district has provided annual
training sessions for teachers, administrators, and support
and classified personnel since the inception of the SBM/
school improvement process. Workshops are held approximately every six weeks. The district also collaborates with
a local university to offer shared decision-making classes
and provides relief-time funds to encourage teachers to attend the classes.

❑ A California school district chose not to provide formal
start-up training to teachers or administrators, but sub-

sequently provided annual in-service workshops for both administrators and teachers. One such training event was an annual supervisional leadership seminar that focused on improving supervisory skills, including problem solving and strategic planning.

❏ Teachers and administrators at an Albuquerque middle school received extensive ongoing in-service training. Although the workshops focused on cooperative learning and other in-structional/curricular practices related to the Re:Learning school approach that the school was adopting, some attention was also paid to decision making and consensus building.

❏ Salt Lake City provided annual training for teachers, other school staff, new site council members, and new school administrators. New site council members and school admin-istrators participated in annual training sessions on shared governance. The district also provided an annual, half-day training session on budgeting and accounting for new prin-cipals, and ongoing training in topics such as team building, consensus building, and meeting management. Schools can also bring in trainers to address their own special needs.

In addition to ongoing workshops, seminars, etc., a number of districts provided written training materials or videotapes to the schools typically on basic concepts and "rules" related to the decentralization effort in that district. Other, more specialized, materials addressed such topics as compliance with the district's decentralized budget system. Such materials could be used for both initial training and "refreshers."

Training Needs

Most school system personnel we interviewed felt that *all* school-level personnel (principals, assistant principals, teachers, and non-certified and classified personnel) needed some training or orientation in SBM theory and principles, whether they were on the site council or not. Some also indicated that site council members should receive specific, more intensive, training since the school-level personnel we interviewed reported that site council members frequently had problems reaching consensus on issues.

Probably the single most important training need we identified was direction in decision sharing for *principals*. This issue came up repeatedly in the schools where SBM did not appear to have produced significant positive effects on science and mathematics education. Many faculty members felt that principals were not sharing responsibility: they gave lip service to SBM, but not substance. Some of the principals we interviewed felt this was a major problem in their district. As justification, the principals we interviewed pointed out that they are held accountable for what happens at their schools, even under SBM. Clearly, principals need training that will encourage them to truly decentralize decision making within their schools. One principal suggested that districts provide SBM principals with a mentor—a principal of a school in which SBM had been successfully implemented—and perhaps even arrange for an "internship" with that principal.

Besides training on basic decision-making themes, an overwhelming majority of the faculty and school administrators who we interviewed indicated that. school-level personnel needed additional, more substantive SBM training in budgeting, accounting or finance, and procurement principles. Many teachers and principals reported that members of site councils, budget committees, and other committees involved with making budgeting and accounting decisions under SBM found the process tedious and time consuming because of their lack of experience and training. A number of the faculty members we interviewed noted that science and mathematics (and other) teachers were reluctant to join site councils or other committees because they felt uncomfortable assuming responsibility for budgeting, procurement, or finance decisions.

In some cases, faculty who were often directly involved in procurement, such as science and mathematics teachers, wanted to play a more aggressive procurement role but were inhibited by their lack of knowledge.

RECOMMENDATIONS

District Level

1. Provide extensive training and "technical" assistance to principals of schools where the district plans to implement SBM. Training should focus on participatory management, supplemented by budgeting, procurement, and personnel issues, and should attempt to alleviate principals' fears of diminishing authority and responsibility under SBM. This effort was most successful, as reported by the principals we interviewed, when they had the opportunity to talk with other principals who had successfully switched to a SBM-type approach.

   Training should also aim to screen out principals who may not be suited for SBM and will be detrimental to the process.

2. Before implementing SBM, provide training to teachers and other school staff in collaborative decision making, consensus building, management techniques, problem solving, trust building and communication, budgeting, accounting, procurement, and preparing vision statements.

   To be effective, training should be provided at the onset of implementation activities—before the establishment of the site council. One respondent noted, "Early training, more training for the entire staff is needed. The district's SBM philosophy and focus should be incorporated in this training; schools need to know what the limitations to their authority will be at the outset. Explain the district's intent and expectations."

3. As a key part of the training, clearly communicate each person's responsibility and authority, including the roles of faculty and department heads in such areas as budgeting, procurement, joint class scheduling, and teaching practices. Spell out any restrictions and limitations imposed by the school and district administration. Encourage department heads and faculty to be innovative.

4. Train central-level personnel (curriculum specialists, accounting staff, middle managers, etc.) to share decision-making authority with school-level personnel so that they will be less likely to impede decentralization efforts through their reluctance to relinquish their authorities.

5. Provide *ongoing* SBM-related training to all school-level personnel (including teachers and school administrators), and especially new personnel who do not come from a SBM school. Material covered should be the same as that for school start-up training. Be sure to clearly include the latest information on responsibilities and authorities. Provide special training in procurement practices for science and mathematics faculty, focusing on their supplies and equipment needs.

6. Provide specialized training to site council members, in addition to that provided for all staff, at the beginning of new council members' tenure. Structure training to emphasize basic decision-making principles and effective communication and trust building between the site council and faculty members and school administrators. Schedule annual ongoing or follow-up training in SBM issues for site council members, focusing on budgeting, finance, and accounting issues.

7. Provide separate SBM training for staff at elementary, middle, and high schools. Some of the faculty we interviewed

indicated that mixed-school training sessions were frustrating and inefficient.

8. Encourage schools to arrange periodic (even annual) sessions on innovations in science and mathematics educational practices, perhaps in association with the science and mathematics specialists at the district administration. These periodic updates will enable science and mathematics teachers to take advantage of SBM's encouragement of innovation to acquire the new software, equipment, and supplies continually emerging in the fast-moving fields of science and mathematics education.

School Level

9. Principals should arrange to provide some training for administrators and teachers in a setting other than the school, such as weekend retreats. Retreats can be highly effective because they are free of school distractions, conducive to breaking down traditional barriers among school personnel, and promote the development of smoother, more effective communication.

10. Principals should send selected teachers and other staff members to other SBM schools to observe their strategies and techniques, learn about their implementation process, and identify problems and their resolutions. This would be particularly useful to schools that are in the planning or early implementation phase of SBM.

CHAPTER 9

Differences between High and Middle/ Junior High Schools

The substantial differences between schools at the middle/junior high and high school levels have substantial implications for decentralization efforts. These differences include size of school, number of students and teachers, curriculum (number and range of subjects taught), and instructional methods used.

FINDINGS

Size and Duration Effects

School level and size (which is closely associated with school level) affect a school's ability to take advantage of decentralization. Middle schools are typically much smaller than high schools in their districts and have smaller budgets and fewer faculty. As a result, these lower level schools usually have fewer options when making trade-offs among budget categories or staff, particularly when state or district requirements such as pupil/teacher ratios are taken into account.

School size also affects the degree of interaction among staff and the time needed to reach decisions. Science and mathematics teachers in one large high school noted that the size of the school (i.e., the number of faculty) complicated and delayed the decision-making process. Indeed, the decision-making process was usually more problematic at the high school level in general than at the middle/junior high school level, primarily because of the number of faculty who needed to communicate and the greater number of steps required in the process (e.g., obtaining input from a greater number of individuals, attempting to work out differences between various parties).

Middle or intermediate schools have their own problems. Since students spend a relatively short amount of time in schools (often only two years), it is—according to one middle school principal—more difficult to generate or sustain parental involvement on their site councils. The resulting rapid parent turnover means that site councils in middle schools have to deal with discontinuity and must "break in" new parent members more frequently than do councils in high schools.

Middle schools generally also have fewer opportunities to offer elective courses than do high schools, thus limiting their potential for innovation and "trying something different." However, because of their greater use of teaching teams, middle schools may afford other opportunities for teacher innovations.

Effects of "Teaching Teams"

A majority of the middle schools we contacted (seven of the nine) had adopted some form of "teaching team" approach to organizing teachers and students within the school. In contrast, this approach was infrequent at the high school level (only 2 of 10 schools). Teaching teams function as a decision-making unit in addition to departments and site councils and thus may be considered a form of decentralization, if not actually a form of SBM.

Under the teaching-team approach, a group of teachers (generally four to six) representing each core subject area are designated as a team (sometimes referred to as a "family"), and a specific group of students are assigned to that team for their core subjects. In some schools, each team and its students are assigned to a specific physical part of the school building, further reinforcing the "team" concept. Members of the teaching team do not necessarily teach any classes together, although there may be some "team teaching" (joint teaching) of specific classes by team members.

A key aspect of teaching teams is that members work together to plan and make decisions about such matters as course content and instructional methods; texts and supplies; and student assignment, progress, and problems. A significant amount of decision making is decentralized to team members in schools using this form of organization. Team members usually are allowed a joint planning period each day (in addition to their individual planning periods) to facilitate group meetings and decision making.

The teaching team approach is a feature of some other teaching "reforms" such as the "Re:Learning" model, which emphasizes interdisciplinary approaches, use of experiential ("hands-on") teaching methods, and cooperative (group) learning. SBM schools we examined that decided to adopt this model also made a commitment to participate in the related training. Two New Mexico middle schools were in the process of becoming Re:Learning schools at the time of our site visits.

Some of the other schools introduced teams because of district-level decisions to implement them in all middle schools. Two junior high/middle schools independently decided to create teaching teams. The Hillsborough junior high school version was a "school-within-a-school," designed to help students with a history of poor grades, disruptive behavior, and inconsistent attendance.

SBM high schools in Prince William County and Prince George's County districts decided to use interdisciplinary teaching teams in both the ninth and tenth grades, in part to facilitate student adjustment to high school. In addition, a Dade County high school introduced a one-year, "school-within-a-school" program for ninth-graders at risk of dropping out (an action the principal felt would have been very difficult without SBM). We found no examples of the use of teaching teams in the eleventh and twelfth grades.

The high school personnel we talked to felt that teaching teams were much more difficult to implement in high schools than in middle schools. The much wider variety of courses, especially in mathematics and science, available in high school makes it very difficult to identify groups of students that could be taught regularly by a core group of faculty. Teaching teams have been successful when limited to special groups of disadvantaged students in the early high school grades.

RECOMMENDATIONS

District Level

1. Since middle and high schools differ so greatly, consider using different SBM models and different degrees of decentralization at the various school levels.

2. Structure training sessions on SBM to reflect these differences. Separate training sessions are likely to be needed for

each school level, at least for all but the most general SBM topics.

3. Encourage the use of the teaching-team model because of its focus on improving curriculum and instruction. Promulgate the innovations made by teaching teams (whether in "regular" or special learning models such as "Re:Learning schools") to other schools, even those that are not formally using teaching teams. This approach is most applicable to middle/junior high schools, but it should be considered for early high school grades, especially to help at-risk students (e.g., the school-within-a-school approach).

School Level

4. In schools that have teaching teams, whether in middle/junior highs or high schools, principals should decentralize budgeting, procurement, personnel, and curriculum/instructional authorities to teams. Take care to ensure that the authorities delegated to different decision-making entities do not clash.

CHAPTER **10**

Roles for School District-Level Science and Mathematics Personnel

The roles of school district-level science and mathematics personnel may be substantially altered under a decentralized system, depending on the extent of delegation to individual schools. In some districts under decentralization, subject supervisors are no longer required to intensively review requests relating to budgets, personnel, equipment, and supplies. What, then, should be their role?

FINDINGS

We found considerable uncertainty among the science and mathematics specialists in the school districts we examined over their new and emerging roles under a decentralized SBM system. Some, as expected, were concerned about their jobs since central specialist positions had been, or were expected to be, eliminated. One respondent said that "these supervisors could no longer walk into schools and make demands;" they had to go through principals or wait to be invited. In effect, their role changed from supervisor to consultant.

The district-level science and mathematics personnel we contacted had usually made only limited efforts at ongoing communication of SBM-related "news" to their teachers—such as which science and mathematics departments were procuring supplies locally (rather than centrally), which schools were developing new curricula or trying new software packages, or which were using new types of equipment and supplies or introducing other innovations. Information, however, occasionally was conveyed in memos to all staff members.

We identified the following roles for district-level science and mathematics specialists under a decentralized SBM system.

❏ Providing information about innovations being tried within the district.

❏ Providing training opportunities to school science and mathematics faculty.

❏ Undertaking regular systematic evaluations of innovative efforts.

❏ Providing technical assistance to schools in evaluating their SBM-related efforts.

Several science and mathematics teachers and school district staff suggested that schools would benefit from receiving such information. Regular communication could promote wider adoption of good practices and innovations, encourage teachers to be more innovative in using the flexibility decentralized to them, and improve attitudes toward SBM procedures by convey-

EXHIBIT 10.1 *Publicizing Innovations: An Example*

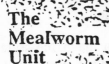

The Mealworm Unit

In this "hands on" discovery science unit, students develop an understanding of the behavior of mealworms. They observe how mealworms react to temperature change, acrid smells, harsh and abrupt sounds, changes in lightness and darkness, and variations in food supply. From their observations, students draw their own conclusions about mealworms by using inductive reasoning.

Students are guided through the process by a worksheet for each day of the three-day unit. The first day they observe how a mealworm moves (is it easier to move uphill or downhill? why?). The second day they observe the mealworms' behavior inside a box (do they climb up the side? do they stand still?). On the third day, they check responses to external stimuli such as vinegar on a cotton swab (can the mealworm smell?), loud noises (can it hear?), and ice cubes (can it feel cold?).

Unlike most science lessons which promote deductive reasoning, this unit enhances inductive reasoning. Students start out with specifics and then derive their own information through discovery and analytical thought. The unit also allows students to express their individualism and creativity.

State and/or District Goals
This unit teaches cause and effect relationships. It encourages students to search for valid and accurate answers to questions.

The Students
More than 100 sixth graders participated. Interest level was high because students actually handled the creatures they studied.

The Staff
Julia Cook teaches science and math at Northwest Intermediate School.

Materials and Facilities
Mealworms, lesson plans, a jar of bran flakes to keep the mealworms in, paper towels, paper and worksheets are needed.

Contact:
Julia Cook
Northwest Intermediate School
1400 Goodwin Ave.
Salt Lake City, UT 84116
(801) 533-3058

Outside Resources
None are needed.

Overall Value
The unit allows students to extrapolate the behavior of mealworms to other animals (transfer of learning). It emphasizes inductive reasoning and encourages students to become actively involved in the learning process. This unit is easy and inexpensive to teach.

Source: 1989 Impact II and Summer Research Grants/1986-89 Salt Lake Education Foundation, April 1990.

ing a sense of shared SBM experience or community (among teachers in different schools).

In some school districts, central-level science and mathematics specialists provided periodic *information about innovations being tried within the district.* For example:

❑ Salt Lake City produced and distributed a magazine-style catalog to teachers to disseminate information about new courses and innovative teaching methods developed by teachers who received summer grants for these purposes. The catalog provided a one-page discussion of each project, including a brief description, information about resources needed to replicate it, and contact information on the teacher who developed it. (Exhibit 10.1 is an example from the catalog.)

❑ Dade County included information about SBM issues and science and mathematics innovations on its district-wide electronic bulletin board. District-level staff also held two district-wide SBM conferences per year. (These conferences were later eliminated, at least temporarily, because of budget cuts.)

❑ In Santa Fe, the superintendent and assistant superintendents met monthly with principals and other school staff to discuss the district's shared decision-making efforts. Schools had the opportunity to raise whatever topics they wished.

District-level science and mathematics specialists usually identified, and sometimes provided, *training opportunities* to school science and mathematics faculty, although most training focused on technical topics rather than SBM-related issues such as group processes. Neither did we find science and mathematics specialists making special efforts to solicit input from school science and mathematics faculty about staff development needs and wishes.

We found no instances of district-level science and mathematics specialists undertaking regular systematic *evaluations of innovative efforts* being made by school faculty. Most, however, did monitor standardized test scores in their subjects and sometimes provided diagnostic feedback to schools on particular areas of weaknesses. Science faculty in one high school emphasized the need for more and better evaluations of new teaching approaches and materials, preferably using robust experimental designs (and not merely, for example, comparing test results at the beginning and end of the trial without an appropriate comparison group).

Another important potential role for school district-level personnel is to provide *technical assistance to schools in evaluating their SBM-related efforts*. A few districts surveyed students, parents, and teachers at each school about their satisfaction with school services. For example, Prince William County and Hillsborough annually administered such surveys and provided each school with its own results, as well as totals for each level (high, middle, or elementary). However, these surveys did not ask about specific subjects (such as science and mathematics), or tabulate the data by department or grade. While school administration personnel found the findings useful, the faculty, including science and mathematics department heads, did not.

RECOMMENDATIONS

District Level

1. School districts should establish ongoing communication of information and "news" relating to SBM in district schools. Procedural issues should be clarified, questions answered, and changes announced. Communication should be a major responsibility of subject specialists. Include in the information descriptions of how particular science or mathematics departments have made new use of their added flexibility,

such as becoming more involved in procuring needed supplies, developing new curricula, trying new software packages, and using new types of equipment or supplies. A separate publication for science and mathematics topics is one option. Another is to provide a separate section on science and mathematics in a general publication. A computerized network might be used to assist this information-sharing activity.

2. School district-level personnel should develop mechanisms to obtain input from schools about problems that require central district administration or inter-school efforts, such as obtaining waivers from district or state requirements on issues that affect more than one school—e.g., use of text books not on district or state lists.

3. District subject specialists should be given the responsibility of seeking input from school faculties about their needs for district in-service staff development programs related to their subjects, such as information about desired content, ways of providing the programs, and who would present them.

4. Central science and mathematics personnel should disseminate information to science and mathematics faculty that evaluates new science and math teaching practices in these areas, including the use of new equipment and software and any other significant innovations. For new practices that are promoted and tried outside the school district, the central staff should assemble and disseminate information including costs, potential accomplishments (preferably based on actual school experiences), benefits, and problems.

School personnel need central personnel to provide objective, impartial advice about technology. Individual teachers are not well positioned to be able to keep up with the latest advances and to evaluate hardware and software, especially long-term costs and other problems.

5. For new practices piloted by one or more of the district's schools, central staff should sponsor, coordinate, and, if necessary, evaluate these new practices. The evaluation should identify costs, problems, ways to alleviate the problems, and outcomes (where possible, covering changes in student achievement and interest), and the piloting teachers' and students' satisfaction with the new practice. Disseminate results clearly, constructively, and reasonably promptly, so that teachers will be stimulated to take advantage of their added flexibility to try new teaching innovations.

   To reduce the cost of such evaluations, central staff might encourage science and mathematics faculty to plan and oversee the individual evaluations, perhaps using students to help with the evaluations as class projects.

6. District-level subject specialists should be given a continuing role in coordinating issues that affect all schools, such as curriculum uniformity across the district, textbook evaluation and adoption, compliance with state and federal regulations, and monitoring of national trends, such as in curriculum and NCTM and NSTA standards.

7. Central science and mathematics staff should periodically (perhaps every year or two) survey science and mathematics faculty about their satisfaction and experiences with SBM-related matters (as well as other science and mathematics issues) to identify problems, solutions (such as needed training), and whether actions are needed at the central level or at individual schools.

8. School districts that decentralize need to consider and plan for the changed roles of district-level science and mathematics specialists. They should not let events just develop or simplistically believe that they do not need these central specialists.

School Level

9. Department heads should serve as links between their faculty members and district subject specialists. They should seek input from their faculties to advise central specialists about needs or problems at the school level.

PART TWO

Effects of SBM Activities

CHAPTER 11

Effects on Teacher Morale and Relationships within the School

Decentralizing authority to schools, departments, and faculty should theoretically increase school staff enjoyment and interest in their work since they have more say in, and control over, their activities. On the other hand, this extra responsibility can also cause conflicts over decisions and place more of a burden on the staff. Difficulties or confusion associated with introducing new forms of decentralization can also negatively impact morale.

OVERALL FINDINGS

We found that the decentralization of decision-making responsibility to the school level had both positive and negative effects on teacher morale and relationships among teachers and administrators. According to many of the school system personnel we interviewed, most teachers in SBM settings were not directly involved in decision making or SBM activities (either by choice or by design) and were not significantly affected by the SBM system. Others reported that the effects of SBM on school climate fluctuated over time. SBM improved the school climate initially by engendering an atmosphere of cooperation and shared responsibility, but this effect was often offset or reversed by internal and external pressures, such as budget cutbacks, teacher frustration about the decision-making process, and administrative changes in the school—e.g., turnover of principals, changes in a new superintendent's perceived level of support for SBM. Many faculty still viewed SBM with suspicion and as a fad that would disappear in time.

Some negative feelings also resulted from other pressures outside the school, such as low wages, reduced budgets, teacher lay-offs, and, in some schools, perceived threats to teachers' physical safety. While not directly related to SBM, these issues affected teacher attitudes in other areas, including SBM.

It should be noted that some SBM schools simultaneously had other types of restructuring efforts in place that also involved decentralization, such as Re:Learning, a school-within-a-school, or a "teaching team" or "family" approach. In such cases, the effects of any one of the decentralization approaches often could not be separated from the others.

Effects on Teacher Morale

While SBM has the potential for increasing teacher morale, faculty in many schools perceived it to have been a mixed blessing. Any effect on teacher morale appeared to depend on how wide a range of teachers (not just a select few) was allowed to participate in the decision-making process (i.e., allowed to vote on a significant number of issues affecting the school) and the extent to which teachers felt that SBM was a force for helping them to do the things they wanted to do. Similarly, morale increased for science and mathematics teachers who were able to introduce changes in teaching methods and gain greater access to resources or supplies because of increased decision-making responsibilities. Morale was also positively affected by the extent to which SBM increased professional development opportunities.

In contrast, teacher morale was negatively affected by the perceived additional uncompensated time faculty felt they had to apply to SBM. Also, conflicts or disagreements arising in conjunction with decentralized decision making had negative effects on the morale of some participants.

■ *EXTENT OF TEACHER INVOLVEMENT IN DECISION MAKING*

Many teachers felt that too little authority was delegated to the school level. Decision areas that teachers were most interested in assuming included curriculum development (developing new curriculum, determining course content changes, selecting textbooks), personnel matters (hiring, staffing, teacher assignments), grading policies, class scheduling, and school schedules. Many of the science and mathematics faculty interviewed were concerned that too few teachers were involved in the decision-making process at their schools.

Decision making at most SBM schools was normally the responsibility of a SBM-created governance body (a site council usually composed of a few teachers, parents, and sometimes the principal), and the principal. However, the principal, in addition to being a member of the site council, typically had the authority to override/veto council decisions and to make decisions without consulting the site council or the school staff. The number of teachers on school governance bodies (site councils, management/school improvement teams) inevitably was small—in the schools we examined, only about eight to nine percent of the teachers served as members of these decision-making bodies. Few teachers who were not council members attended the meetings, although in most schools, they were welcome. A better measure of teacher morale was the proportion of faculty who felt they had access to the council and the proportion of teachers who felt their views were not adequately represented.

Some schools used special strategies to incorporate a broader base of teachers and other school staff into the decision-making process; and to make teachers feel more empowered. These included:

❑ Creating sub- or ad hoc committees (budget, curriculum, staff development, etc.), primarily composed of teachers, that functioned as advisory or adjunct decision-making groups.

❑ Allowing the whole faculty to vote on issues that were particularly important or had school-wide implications. An Albuquerque high school used a full-faculty vote to approve a new attendance policy, and a Santa Fe high school allowed the whole staff to participate in deciding where to make state- or district-mandated cutbacks in the school budget.

❑ Allowing all departments within the school to discuss decisions before a final decision was made by the site council.

❑ Abolishing department head positions and delegating decision-making responsibilities for the department to its teachers.

Teacher support for SBM and teacher morale was higher in those schools in which one of these additional decision-making strategies were used *and* when teachers felt they had been given the opportunity to be directly involved in decision making. Correspondingly, teacher pessimism and skepticism about the effectiveness, utility, and success of SBM programs fell according to their perceptions of their opportunities for participation.

❑ In a Fort Worth middle school, the principal reported that teachers felt more in control and were happier because they were sharing decision making. They were "buying into the business." Science and mathematics faculty reported that the school's instructional team approach had a significant positive impact on teacher morale, and noted that the teams' common planning time provided opportunities for support and sharing. (Teachers used planning periods to discuss student problems, jointly develop lesson plans, schedules, etc.)

The mathematics and science departments at this school were very receptive to SBM and were able to use its flexibility features to implement a number of curricula changes quickly. For example, the school converted participation in mathematics and science projects from a voluntary activity to a compulsory activity for all students.

❑ Mathematics and science department heads in an Adams County Twelve Five Star district high school felt that SBM had at least indirectly contributed to positive changes in teacher motivation and enthusiasm, as evidenced by their increased interest in attending professional development seminars, taking a certification course that allowed them to conduct teacher evaluations, taking refresher or continuing education courses, and attending training seminars offered by the state or district.

❑ Science and mathematics teachers and department heads in a Prince George's County high school were ambivalent about SBM's effects on teacher morale. Some teachers were enthusiastic because under SBM, they had flexibility and autonomy to use more innovation and creativity in their teaching methods. But these teachers reported that many of the other teachers in the school felt they were inadequately involved in decision making for the school.

❑ Some faculty who were not on the site council felt somewhat isolated from the SBM experience in several schools. Teachers wanted more information about what went on in school management team meetings, what and how decisions were made, and what options were considered.

Teacher morale was also affected by the amount of decision-making authority that was delegated to the school and the degree of visible change that took place within the school as a result of SBM implementation. Science and mathematics teachers at schools that received substantive decision-making authority over a range of areas—such as budgeting, hiring, curriculum, instructional methods, attendance policies, grading policies, class scheduling, student placement—generally were more enthusiastic about and supportive of SBM than teachers in schools with only limited and/or superficial decision-making authorities.

■ *TIME REQUIRED FOR SBM ACTIVITIES*

SBM had negative effects on teacher morale when they felt that excessive time demands were placed on them to participate in SBM activities (site council, committee meetings, etc.), sometimes at the expense of their other teaching responsibilities. Many of the SBM schools that we examined conducted decision-making activities during lunch periods, before school began, or after school, since school districts did not usually allow SBM schools to alter school schedules so that decision-making meetings could take place during regular school hours. Nor was relief time allocated to encourage teachers to increase their participation in SBM. Many of the science and mathematics teachers reported making considerable personal sacrifices to participate in and sustain SBM programs at their school.

The failure of some school districts to allow sufficient flexibility in school and teaching schedules diminishes teacher support for SBM and to some degree undermines one of the primary objectives of the decentralization movement: to increase the involvement of teachers in making decisions that affect their schools. Many teachers reported that they felt burdened by the additional responsibilities they assumed when participating in SBM. They felt that the time and attention they devoted to governance, administrative, and collaborative issues had diverted their time and attention away from basic teaching responsibilities (such as developing lesson plans, grading papers, and meeting with or tutoring students).

Some of the science and mathematics faculty interviewed felt that teachers should be financially compensated for their additional responsibilities and time commitments under SBM. In their view, the absence of financial compensation had caused or exacerbated teachers' lack of interest and non-participation in SBM. A few schools reimbursed teachers for time devoted to management, such as site council meetings. For example, an Albuquerque middle school provided teachers a stipend of $15.40 per hour for their participation in management council meetings. They were paid out of a restructuring grant that the school received.

■ EFFECTS ON THE PROFESSIONAL DEVELOPMENT OF TEACHERS

SBM had a positive effect on teacher morale and support and enthusiasm for SBM if their schools thereby gained greater authority to make decisions that directly affected and enhanced the professional development opportunities of teachers, such as teacher attendance at and participation in educational workshops, professional meetings, and seminars.

Most schools indicated they had been offered a wide range of in-service training events since SBM, some of which were related to other restructuring movements such as Re:Learning or Essential schools, or to team teaching methods and styles.

In addition, many science and mathematics teachers we interviewed reported that SBM had increased their opportunities to attend a wide range of training events, including university-, state-, and association-sponsored meetings, workshops, and seminars. (We do not know the extent to which the added science and mathematics training resulted from Eisenhower grant funds and not SBM; we suspect that some had.) Some schools used SBM flexibility to allocate funds to sponsor teacher participation in training events, to pay for substitutes so that they could participate in events held during school hours, and to institute liberal leave policies that permitted and encouraged teacher attendance and participation in such events.

❑ The Adams County Twelve Five Star school district instituted a liberal "Professionals Day" policy that allowed teachers to attend workshops or seminars. The costs of attendance at these seminars and of hiring substitute teachers to replace them were paid out of department budgets.

❑ A Prince George's County high school encouraged staff to attend development activities, offering a stipend of $75 a day for participation. To supplement these funds, some department heads within the school sought additional grants from the National Science Foundation.

Most science and mathematics teachers felt attendance at such seminars was invaluable, enabling them to keep abreast of curricula and instructional reforms taking place throughout the country (such as those being advocated by the National Council of Teachers of Mathematics and the National Science Teachers Association), and to enhance their knowledge of their disciplines. For example, some mathematics teachers credited SBM with giving them the opportunity to attend professional meetings sponsored by NCTM. Others credited SBM with making available the in-service funds that allowed them to attend regional mathematics conferences. According to one mathematics department head, opportunities for professional development increased within the district because SBM school administrations were more supportive in providing funds for attendance at professional meetings and conferences.

Science teachers were somewhat less positive about the linkage between SBM and increased opportunities to attend professional workshops or conferences, but the difference may have been due to the promulgation of the new NCTM guidelines during this time.

Another area of professional growth that SBM reportedly opened for science and mathematics teachers was increased participation in grant solicitation and proposal writing. High school science departments, in particular, became increasingly active in seeking grant funding to meet gaps in education funds and as a means of acquiring state-of-the-art technology (computers, software packages) and other costly innovative instructional materials and supplies (graphing calculators, etc.).

Effects on Intra-School Relationships

■ *RELATIONS BETWEEN FACULTY AND THE PRINCIPAL*

Faculty members frequently reported that the relationship between the principal and faculty was critical to success of SBM. In many of the schools we contacted, the current principal was credited with most of the SBM-related improvements.

In some schools, however, the relationship between the school principals and other members of the school staff seemed to have been negatively impacted by SBM implementation. Some teachers and principals reported that SBM had caused a strain in the relationship between principals and various members of the school staff, particularly when: a) principals overturned or vetoed site council decisions; and b) principals made an excessive number of decisions without seeking input from the site council, committees, or the faculty. A principal exercising these prerogatives was perceived by school staff as autocratic and unwilling to share decision-making authority. In some cases, teachers who felt they had had a special relationship with the principal, and, therefore, informal influence on decision making, were upset that they had been displaced by the site council.

By and large, we found that relationships between teachers in the same or different departments, between teachers and department heads, and between teachers and students and their parents were not significantly affected by SBM. However, respondents at some schools, especially those that were using team teaching or subject-integration practices, reported some improvement in information sharing and curriculum/instructional collaboration between teachers and departments. (These efforts were often introduced as part of other restructuring movements and were not necessarily related to SBM, particularly in middle schools.)

■ *RELATIONS AMONG SCHOOL PERSONNEL*

In a few instances, we found some friction and disagreement between members of the site council and non-council members who saw particular council decisions as self- or department-promoting and not representative of the wishes of the majority of the faculty. A few faculty felt that SBM had pitted department against department and teacher against teacher. Some teachers who had been actively involved in SBM activities believed that cronyism/elitism was preventing all but a small, select group of teachers from participating in decision making.

Increased participation of faculty and other staff in decision making sometimes led to conflict and a negative impact on morale for some individuals. Faculty and other staff who had not previously participated in group decision making processes did not always handle dissension decision making in a positive way.

❏ When science faculty in one school expressed concerns about particular changes under consideration, other faculty members treated them as obstacles to change "as if they were the bad guys." Possibly as a result, science faculty in that school seemed less enthusiastic about SBM than the mathematics faculty, who had no similar negative experiences.

❏ In two middle schools that adopted teaching-team approaches, faculty members had difficulty maintaining cordial and cooperative relationships with each other in group decision-making situations. Both of these schools used their increased budget flexibility to provide training in interpersonal communication and decision-making skills to alleviate these problems. In both cases, the school's response resolved the initial communication problems, and morale was not negatively affected in the long run.

■ *COLLABORATION AMONG TEACHERS*

In some schools, SBM led to more collaboration, not only within the same subject department but also across departments. This was particularly the case for site council members but was also reported by several other mathematics and science teachers. One principal felt that the needs assessments conducted by the site council was the first opportunity faculty had to exchange views and problems, particularly about budget issues.

In other schools, teachers collaborated on budget issues, such as deferring purchase of textbooks in one department to provide funds for purchasing whole sets of books in another department.

The most common form of collaboration occurred within teaching teams in middle schools, and included sharing of instructional and non-instructional duties. For example, all members of a team would meet with parents of problem students. Teachers of different subjects would also sometimes combine elements of their subjects to help students. For example, teachers of reading cooperated with mathematics teachers to include mathematics vocabulary activities as part of a reading lesson. This trend toward thematic integrated teaching, while encouraged by SBM, is probably more heavily influenced by national trends toward integration between and within subjects, such as that embodied in the NCTM standards. Nevertheless, SBM and teaching-team procedures appeared to be speeding up this process.

RECOMMENDATIONS

Many of the concerns voiced to us focused on the need for schools, principals, and school districts to develop and implement policies and practices that would increase the level of teacher/school staff interest and participation in SBM and promote increased intra-school cooperation and collaboration.

District Level

1. School districts should delegate sufficient decision-making responsibility to schools to promote and sustain teacher/ school staff interest in and support for SBM, and to reduce some of the cynicism and pessimism of school staff toward SBM. Clearly communicate the added flexibility and responsibility to school personnel.

2. School districts should involve school-level representatives (teachers, administrators) in district-wide committees or task forces such as central-level curricula committees, to gain schools' acceptance of the changes.

3. School districts should reduce the hardships teachers and other school-level personnel undergo to participate in SBM, by granting schools the flexibility to schedule time for SBM meetings and other business during regular school hours (not necessarily during lunch periods)—for example, by extending planning periods or allowing schools to use half a day a month for whole faculty meetings. A budget category might be created to compensate teachers for the additional time they devote to certain, non-routine SBM activities.

4. School districts should support sufficient staff/professional development opportunities by giving schools the flexibility to use available funds to sponsor frequent in-service teacher training and teacher attendance at workshops and seminars. Allow schools to institute liberal leave policies that permit and encourage teacher attendance at these events. The costs of substitute teachers likely can be alleviated somewhat by allowing teachers the flexibility to work out coverage arrangements with their fellow teachers. Here, as elsewhere, SBM should be used to enable schools to tap into teacher ingenuity.

School Level

5. Principals and site councils should encourage and broaden teacher involvement in SBM. Consider such options as: a) presenting major issues to the full faculty for a vote; b) involving as many of the staff as possible in decision making, not just the more motivated, enthusiastic teachers; and c) in general, establishing an atmosphere where teacher input is welcome and teachers feel their ideas are valued even though they may not result in school policy or administrative changes.

6. Principals and site councils should promote better communication within the school to increase the teachers' sense of SBM involvement. Encourage site council representatives to seek *input* from all staff they are representing (e.g., science and mathematics representatives should seek input from all faculty in their departments), and to provide prompt and thorough *feedback* to those they represent on council activities and decisions (in writing or orally). Teachers not on the site council need more information about that goes on in school management meetings. Material in addition to meeting minutes is needed to brief the faculty at large on site council activities and help make them feel they are part of, or at least knowledgeable about, the process.

7. Principals and department heads should encourage innovative teachers to help other teachers within the school. A major professional development opportunity, and one that seems to be considerably underused in the schools we examined, lies in giving science and mathematics faculty in-depth information and exposure to new teaching approaches (new to the school), such as the use of software programs and various equipment. Often new approaches were brought in by, and for, one adventurous faculty member. Other faculty teaching the same subjects should *tactfully* be given the opportunity to learn how to use the approaches or tools from a colleague. Except where strong evidence exists that current methods are ineffective, other

faculty should not be forced to use the "new" teaching approaches but should be given constructive encouragement.

8. School districts and their schools should provide training to faculty in group decision making, team building, and communication skills. This can alleviate or avert hostilities and negative impacts on morale that occasionally occur under decentralized decision making.

CHAPTER 12

SBM Effects on Accountability

We asked respondents if SBM had changed the level of accountability for school performance in the school as a whole, in the science and mathematics departments, or among individual faculty. We also asked whether the form or content of individual evaluations had changed.

Our primary concern was whether accountability had changed because of SBM, or whether schools with SBM were held more or less accountable than non-SBM schools in the district. We found little change.

School accountability can take many forms. Schools may have to demonstrate compliance with financial regulations or with procedural guidelines and policies, improvements in educational performance (usually measured by students' test scores), or they may be subject to more subjective judgments. Ways to demonstrate accountability can also vary greatly, from simple reports to elaborate systems of rewards or sanctions for reaching or failing to reach certain goals or targets. We found examples of each of these kinds of accountability in the schools in our sample.

FINDINGS

Changes in School Accountability

In most districts, no additional accountability requirements were *imposed* on SBM schools. (Many of them were already required to produce annual reports.) Any additional requirements most often took the form of an annual report by the school or the site council. These reports were most often "low stakes," intended to serve as a source of information and as input for the next year's planning. The exception was in Hillsborough County, where a private company sponsored a competition for the "best" SBM programs and awarded the winning school $30,000.

In our sample, two schools reported that they were conducting structured evaluations of some of their SBM programs on their own initiative, but in general, districts did not mandate formal evaluations of SBM programs (nor of specific educational changes) as part of the reporting process.

❑ The site improvement council of a Salt Lake City high school prepared reports on its activities and expenditures. Anybody receiving money also had to prepare a report, which was supposed to show growth or advancement. Budget accountability also led to a focus on indicators, such as student attendance. For example, the council was supposed to indicate in its report the extent to which attendance had improved and demonstrate that the money was well spent. "Shared governance means that what people do is very transparent. A lot of this comes from a sense that you need to produce."

Only one district seems to have significantly altered the district-wide school accountability requirements coincident with introducing SBM. Santa Fe sought to evaluate schools on the following criteria: a) improved student performance; b) compliance with district standards for mission/vision; c) compliance with requirements of state and federal law and school board policies; and d) effective use of resources.

SBM schools in two other districts sought to modify externally mandated standardized test requirements. (Other districts were also loosening testing requirements for all schools, independent of SBM, because of budget cuts or doubts about the inappropriateness of the tests, or as part of the larger movement towards performance tests.)

❑ A Bellevue middle school was able to test only once a year, instead of the three or four times, by combining several assessment tests and administering them at the same time.

❑ Chemistry and biology teachers at a Salt Lake City high school decided that the annual district testing was inadequate and ill-timed and, therefore, had no diagnostic or remediation value. They asked the district to allow a committee of interested teachers to develop better tests to be given twice a year.

Several schools took advantage of decentralized authority to change the way they assessed their students (independent of district reforms).

❑ A Poway high school introduced portfolio assessment in upper level physics.

❑ A Santa Fe high school changed its assessment practices to incorporate lab reports as a major part of students' grades. The mathematics department also tried to use "buddy exams" (where two or more students worked on an assignment) as part of their hands-on, performance-based teaching approach.

❑ The science department of a Kalispell high school developed guidelines to change the student performance assessments to include more practical exams, more oral exams, and more essays. The mathematics department used buddy exams and more project-oriented assessments.

❑ The science department of a Dade high school developed a competency-based program in biology that included a testing program based on a standardized curriculum. Students had to demonstrate mastery of the material covered every nine weeks. This school-developed program deviated from past district practice. Teachers said that the testing program would probably have been developed anyway as part of a district-wide trend to develop a competency-based curriculum, but SBM fostered experimentation and allowed faster implementation.

❑ A Santa Fe middle school developed and received a waiver for a series of "exit competencies." The state also began using the series as a model for statewide competencies for its Re:Learning program. Competency checklists identified the skills students needed to move to the next level or areas where remediation or acceleration was appropriate. However, students still received grades and were examined in all subjects.

While schools and school districts all kept a close eye on student test scores, few, if any, appeared to be systematically tracking either how well the SBM decentralization process was working or the effects on students (and teachers) of decentralization-related activities or projects (such as new science or mathematics curricula, new science software, new math manipulatives, etc.). Nor did we find that individual SBM science and mathematics departments undertook special assessment efforts.

An occasional exception was the administration of surveys, especially by the school district. At least two districts, Hillsborough and Prince William Counties, annually surveyed students, parents, and teachers to obtain feedback on a variety of school characteristics (e.g., safety, discipline, fairness). The results were tabulated by school and disseminated to each school, and were used primarily by the principal and assistants. However, since the questions asked in the surveys were not related to specific subject areas, the feedback was not directly useful to science and mathematics department heads or their faculties.

On the whole, we found no major changes in the way in which SBM schools were held accountable for financial or other decisions or for student progress.

Changes in Evaluations of Individuals

The selections below discuss the "accountability" process for persons in each of three categories: principals, teachers, and parents who were site council members.

■ *PRINCIPALS' ACCOUNTABILITY*

Principals in 7 of the 19 schools we examined said that there had been no change in the way they were held accountable, including the way they were evaluated. In four schools, principals said they felt more accountable, even though the district's requirements had not changed. Several principals said that the additional people involved in the decision-making process (especially the budget) meant that they had to justify and defend their every decision, and undergo more questioning of their decisions by teachers and parents. This was welcome for some, but a source of conflict for others.

❏ In a Salt Lake City high school, the SBM program was constantly evaluated informally. Two school board members came to the School Community Council (SCC) meetings, and were the first to inform the principal of any problems.

Only three districts substantially changed the way principals were evaluated as a result of SBM.

❏ The Santa Fe district held principals accountable for decisions made by the schools, and the district evaluated them on their SBM performance. SBM evaluation criteria included the principals' work with SBM and their ability to work collaboratively in a SBM setting. Their ratings were based on teacher surveys of the principal's performance and if, and how, the principal practiced collaborative management. However, a high school principal said that while the evaluation criteria were different, SBM had not significantly increased his accountability.

❏ Also in Santa Fe, the district added questions about SBM to the principals' and assistant principals' evaluation instrument, which enabled them to obtain teachers' perceptions of their performance.

❏ The principal of an Adams County Twelve Five Star district high school said that she was held accountable by the central office and school board for the decisions made for the school. However, she also said that shared decision making spread accountability among other school personnel, so that she did not feel she stood alone. Other SBM principals also noted that they spoke for the whole faculty now when arguing with the central office or school board.

Principals in some schools were concerned because they were held accountable for the decisions of others, yet under SBM, they had limited power over decisions with which they disagreed.

■ *TEACHER ACCOUNTABILITY*

Only three districts modified teacher evaluations to account for SBM-related changes in teachers' roles. This was generally true for department heads, also, even though in some cases, their responsibility for budget matters had changed considerably. However, in two schools, department heads were no longer appointed by the principal; they were elected annually by the faculty. Both said that their success at re-election was one additional evaluation criterion. Examples of how teacher evaluations changed include the following:

❑ In a Kalispell high school, teachers were observed and evaluated separately by both the principal and department head. Teachers could not be involved more directly in the evaluation process because only state-certified staff could actually conduct evaluations. However, teachers could and did suggest modifications to the evaluation forms used, leading to the use of more narrative in the forms instead of the previous checklist format.

❑ Department heads at the Kalispell high school had the primary responsibility for budget development for their departments. They sought and incorporated the advice of teachers in making budget decisions but ultimately were held solely accountable for their departments' budget requests and purchases, which were monitored by the principal and department chair committee. Department heads also acted as the spokespersons for their departments on the department chair committee and were responsible to their departments for decisions made by the committee. Not all department heads appreciated this accountability.

❑ A Santa Fe middle school was in the process of developing a plan to give teachers a role in determining performance factors for teacher evaluations. The teachers would also participate in conducting evaluations (currently done by the principal and assistant principal). The plan had to be approved by the district. The principal also felt that school administrators were more amenable to questioning by parents, teachers, and students. The past district and state practice of surveying teacher and parent attitudes had not changed.

Despite overall positive effects, some teachers felt uncomfortable with the additional responsibility and were worried that their evaluations could be affected by their inability or unwillingness to assume additional responsibility. One teacher commented that she was more apprehensive about losing her job now than before SBM.

❑ A Bellevue middle school made some changes in the content of individual annual performance evaluations to consider the extent to which teachers were involved in the whole school and not just the classroom (e.g., their attendance at in-service courses, involvement in the action council).

❑ Poway's district-wide mandated policy for evaluating teachers, specified in teachers' contracts, stated that the principal or assistant principal had responsibility for conducting the evaluations, but under SBM, teachers could have input into determining the criteria on which they were rated. Teachers with five or more years of experience could also choose an alternative evaluation procedure in which they were rated on a project they had completed in lieu of the traditional evaluation criteria. However, the principal at each school decided if and what types of alternative evaluation measures could be used and which teachers could opt for it. To evaluate teachers with less than three years experience, school staff could use a peer assistance procedure in which a group of teachers from the district assisted the principal in observing teachers.

Teachers in several schools said that shared decision making increased their accountability. In several cases where teachers had more control over budget decisions, there was also evidence that they were more cost conscious, were more concerned about getting the best value for the money spent, and sought out cheaper sources of supply.

❑ In a Fort Worth middle school, standardized test results were one of the direct means by which SBM effectiveness was judged. If money was spent in a certain area, these tests were closely examined to see if the funds were producing results. Teachers interviewed also reported feelings of increased professional accountability. One said, "Accountability seems to be increasing each year. When you take more responsibility you have to be accountable. We have to keep checking on ourselves—ask the reasons why certain kids are failing. This is encouraged within the teams. In the future, the SBM process will have to be even more open. Priorities will have to be agreed to, and all teachers will need to be involved or else people will start to get disillusioned."

■ *ACCOUNTABILITY OF PARENTS ON THE SITE COUNCIL*

A small number of schools expressed concern about the accountability of parents who were members of site councils. The issue arose because parents can become members of site councils in different ways: by invitation or appointment of the principal, by virtue of executive posts they held in the school's PTA, or by election from the parent body at large. Therefore, the schools questioned the extent to which these parents represented any constituency, how they obtained input from other parents, and how they communicated decisions to others. Parent site-council members who represented PTAs usually presented oral or written reports to members at annual or monthly meetings as a means of accounting for their involvement. Parents in another district used a phone-tree system to sample community views. However, the schools that raised this issue believed that neither solution was totally adequate.

An interesting twist on the accountability dimension concerns the accountability of parents. Several middle schools and at least one high school said that the student discipline policies they had adopted under SBM and teaching teams, placed greater responsibilities on parents—for example, by requiring them to come to the school to meet with the faculty (usually the whole team responsible for the student) when the student was in trouble.

RECOMMENDATIONS

Readers should note that the issues of accountability and personnel evaluation have legal and contractual ramifications that extend beyond the boundaries of any one school and are beyond the scope of this report. However, several points are clear from the experience of the districts in this study:

1. School districts and individual schools should revise principal and teacher annual performance evaluation criteria to reflect the differences in the roles and responsibilities of the principal and teachers under SBM. (Most districts have not faced this issue yet.) They might, for example, include an evaluation criterion on the extent to which principals and teachers make collaborative decisions and innovate in their work (trying different ways to deliver science and mathematics education).

2. Reinforce the school's commitment to shared decision making by giving teachers input in determining the evaluation procedure.

3. In the spirit of school-centered decision making, schools should not require individual faculty to participate in group activities. Some faculty may work best as individuals, and should be permitted to do so without penalty. SBM should not mean that all faculty have to be involved in group efforts for every decision.

4. If SBM is intended to increase parent input, schools should conduct regular (perhaps annual) surveys of parents. Ask parents for their perceptions as to their own ability to provide input and obtain information provided on school and site council activities. To obtain information of use to science and mathematics (and other) departments, parents should be asked subject-specific questions. The school site council might be the "sponsor" of the survey.

5. Science and mathematics departments should sponsor regular, perhaps annual, surveys of their students and students' parents, even if their school does not. The survey should seek information on perceptions of the quality of the science and mathematics education, including the value and utility

of equipment, facilities, extra-curricular activities, class size, and course content and instruction. Such information not only would provide an accountability tool, but more importantly, could guide science and mathematics faculties to make needed improvements. While such an effort is appropriate in non-SBM schools as well, the decentralized environment of SBM should be more conducive to this procedure and be less threatening to faculty. Also, science and mathematics faculties in SBM schools are likely to be better able than other faculties (having more flexibility) to use the feedback to improve science and mathematics education.

CHAPTER 13

SBM Effects on Science and Mathematics Curricula and Instruction

A key concern for science and mathematics educators and others interested in the state of science and mathematics education is how decentralization has benefited education and in what ways.

As noted in the introduction, this study was primarily concerned with investigating the extent to which school-based management efforts affected science and mathematics education, and to a lesser extent, how SBM affected outcomes for students. However, science and mathematics education encompasses complex interactions between school organizational structures; state, district, and local school policies; the content of instruction; teaching styles; and interpersonal dynamics. A full analysis of all these interactions with SBM in all its forms was beyond the scope of this study. We therefore limited our focus of science and mathematics education to two areas: what is taught, including the curriculum and textbook selection, and how it is taught. We asked respondents only about changes to mathematics and science education, although other subject areas may have also changed.

Besides changes to curriculum, textbook choice, and instructional practices, we also include in this chapter a brief section on the dangers of introducing too many innovations at one time.

FINDINGS

Changes to Mathematics and Science Curricula

SBM has not had major impacts on mathematics and science *curricula* as yet: 14 of the 19 schools studied reported that district or state requirements largely determined their curricula (e.g., guidelines, frameworks, objectives, standardized tests). However, many science and mathematics departments were able to adopt some changes recommended by their own faculty. Within limits, most schools and their departments had some autonomy over *course offerings*, *course content*, and *the sequencing of material within courses*, either on their own authority or after approval from the district.

Many schools were able to make these kinds of decisions prior to SBM, but SBM led to changes in who makes the decisions, how they are made, and how quickly changes could be made. For example, the initiative to introduce a new course, which would have been made by the principal or other administrator before SBM, was made by departments or a school-wide curriculum committee in a SBM school.

❑ Two schools in our sample, both from New Mexico, departed radically from past practice in terms of curriculum, as a result of their participation in a wider Re:Learning/Essential Schools initiative, a decision that was school-based.

Other than these two cases, principals and faculty who we interviewed reported that curriculum decisions were easier with SBM than before because SBM created a climate conducive to change and experimentation.

Teachers in several schools noted that while there had not yet been any substantial changes in curriculum, they had become more aware of the need to change and less accepting of the status quo, and had begun discussing possibilities for doing things differently.

❑ While curriculum is set by the county, teachers in one high school said they had always had freedom in how to teach. Mathematics teachers were bound by class sequencing (e.g., algebra 1, geometry, algebra 2), but some wanted to be able to alter the sequence or to develop mathematics courses geared more to their students (e.g., a nine-week elective course on the techniques of graphing). Mathematics teachers said that, if nothing else, being able to make these decisions would make them feel better about themselves and more professional. Science teachers said that they had discussed different ways of doing things under SBM, such as having smaller lab classes and larger discussion classes, and more health-oriented or more use-oriented courses for students at the lower level. Before SBM, they would not have even held discussions because they felt unable to effect any change.

❑ A group of science and mathematics teachers in the Hillsborough school district told us, "We would like to be able to rearrange the school day, adjust course outlines, have more interaction among the disciplines—for example, longer science lab periods and advanced mathematics and computer labs. We would like to teach less, but teach better rather than giving superficial coverage."

SBM, particularly the philosophy of shared decision making, brought some important changes to the way that curriculum was determined at the district level. This is especially important in smaller districts, where there may be only a few high schools.

❑ At a Salt Lake City high school, teachers were given more opportunities to become involved in curriculum development committees. The district made considerable effort to distribute draft versions of curriculum revisions (such as a new reading curriculum) to all teachers in the district for comment before final adoption. The individual schools decided, in part, which teachers would serve on these committees.

❑ Teachers in the Poway school system had input to curriculum decisions through their participation in a district-wide curriculum committee, which acted as an advisory body to the central staff in suggesting and effecting curriculum change. Through this committee, teachers were able to bring about changes in courses offered, course content, and textbooks selected. For example, the committee was able to change the content of an algebra/geometry course offered at both the middle and high school level so as to bridge the two levels.

About half of the schools surveyed said that they had been able to modify courses they offered, at least in part because of the SBM process.

❑ Three middle schools introduced algebra or pre-algebra courses (or made them available to the majority of students rather than select individuals).

❑ Two schools re-introduced lower level courses. A Hillsborough middle school altered the county requirement that all students take pre-algebra to allow students in a drop-out prevention program to take general math.

❑ An Adams County Twelve Five Star district also replaced an algebra class with basic mathematics.

Some high schools obtained waivers from the district to alter graduation requirements.

Several of the schools we surveyed made changes to strengthen requirements.

❑ A Dade County high school required all students to take four credits/years of mathematics to graduate, whereas the district and the state required only three credits. Mathematics was made compulsory for all students in the school, including seniors, resulting in a very large number of mathematics classes. Teachers had input into this decision, and teachers, not administrators, decided what courses to offer.

❑ A Prince William County high school discontinued a general mathematics course because the school/department thought that the standard was too low. One teacher said, "If students haven't learned it by high school they probably never will. Instead we offer a more practical, applied course."

❑ An Albuquerque high school mathematics department also eliminated basic math from its curriculum. The department initiated a departmental final exam for Algebra I as part of an outcomes-based program.

❑ At the insistence of the mathematics teachers, the Kalispell high school increased the number of advanced-level mathematics courses, offering two full sections of calculus, for example, rather than one. The basic math 2 and math 3 courses changed to blend in mathematical functions incorporating graphing, and courses were more technology focused than in the past.

Schools that developed or introduced new courses most often did so to draw on the particular talents of the teachers in the school at the particular time.

❑ A Salt Lake City high school added an aviation course proposed by a member of the science faculty (a former pilot), opening up an area of interest for students who might not otherwise have been exposed to the level of learning and certain mathematical and scientific concepts (such as weather patterns). Students were required to take the FAA exam as their final exam for the course, earning them impressive credentials and emphasizing the concrete linkage between education and the real world.

This school also established an astronomy course, using a new teacher who had skills in astronomy. Likewise, a science teacher at the school was developing a wildlife biology course in conjunction with the Bureau of Land Management, Forestry Department, and Utah State University. As a science teacher at the school said, "Teachers have great flexibility to introduce topics and courses so long as they fit the core objectives."

Faculty at this school also decided that the technical and vocational education curriculum was not meeting the needs of the students, so they developed their own and established an "Academy of Technology." Students were required to have good grades in the basic subjects to enroll. These courses earned concurrent credit with the high school and community college, counting toward graduation in both institutions. Teachers from the school were also accepted as adjunct staff at the college. These activities were initiated within the department and endorsed by the School Improvement Council.

❏ A Santa Fe high school science department introduced a new science course entitled "Science for Today's World," a ninth-grade course added as a prerequisite for biology, chemistry, and physics.

❏ Prior to SBM, a central curriculum supervisor decided on the curriculum in Prince William County, advised by four or five selected teachers over the summer. School staff interviewed felt that the supervisors did not pay sufficient attention to the needs of individual schools. Under SBM, the teachers and the principal within the school made the decisions about course content and course offerings, guided by state course requirements and subject to approval by the board of education. For example, the school developed a one-semester advanced probability and statistics course, the first in the county. Other schools in the district later adopted the course. As another example, the science department prepared curriculum plans for astronomy, geology, and oceanographic courses, soon to be offered to students. Sometimes curriculum development was a cooperative venture with teachers from three to four nearby schools. Departments did not get any extra funding to offer these new courses. The enrollment in the new courses reduced enrollments in other courses, but this was seen to have stimulated some productive discussion among the faculty on the values and merits of one course versus another (e.g., physics versus geology). These courses might have been offered without SBM, but they were implemented more quickly under SBM because staff, students, and parents were all involved.

Other SBM schools introduced new courses intended to fill the needs of their particular students or remedy weaknesses in the existing curriculum.

❏ In an Albuquerque high school, curriculum changes were normally discussed first in department meetings, then presented to the curriculum committee by the department head (the curriculum committee here consisted of all department heads) and acted on by the committee or the management council. Suggestions for curricular change were overseen by central-level personnel if waivers or policy changes were required. Prior to SBM implementation, any school-based curriculum decisions were made by the principal and assistant principals, not by faculty.

❏ At a Prince William County SBM middle school, faculty began discussing how to make students better learners. As a result, they established new keyboarding and computer operations courses. Teachers were paid from school funds to work over the summer to develop detailed lesson plans for these courses.

❑ A Bellevue middle school developed a pilot environmental science course for the sixth-grade in 1992. After review, the school decided to offer it in the seventh and eighth grades. Also, an advanced life science course was developed for the eighth grade. The development of these courses exemplified what the principal saw as the main role of SBM: everybody in the school participating in discussing and thinking about what students needed in science, how the material related to other subjects, and determining which courses to offer. This school also decided to "untrack;" that is, it switched from several mathematics courses at each level before SBM to only one mathematics course in the sixth-grade and two courses (basic and advanced) in the eighth grade.

❑ A Dade County middle school introduced an elective environmental science course. Even though it was discontinued when district-level cutbacks forced the school into a six-period day, the principal believed that the effort had changed the mind set of teachers and had encouraged them to try new things in mathematics, such as establishing a research elective and allowing some sixth-grade students to take pre-algebra. The school also offered summer courses for these advanced students so that they could take honors algebra in the seventh grade.

❑ At a Poway high school, science teachers had significant input into the course content of a new physical science class to be offered to all freshman across the district. All teachers in the school had the opportunity to be involved in this activity. The development was a joint effort by teachers from all three schools in the district to standardize the content, to adopt a thematic approach to teaching the class, and to select the textbook.

A license to be flexible seemed to be the advantage of SBM most often cited by teachers. Science and mathematics faculty enthusiasm seemed highly related to their degree of participation in determining which direction was best.

Two schools mentioned special problems concerning SBM and curriculum. Teachers in one school said that, while they had input into the overall program, they no longer had time to meet and discuss particular subject issues. As one noted, "Morning time is taken up by committee meetings of one kind or other, and the afternoon is taken up by the activity program. SBM has siphoned too much time away from curriculum issues into whole school issues. It has been negative in this respect." In another school, teachers were frustrated that their attempts to make curriculum changes had been blocked by the district—for example, the mathematics department's attempt to introduce a probability/statistics course at the pre-algebra level. A proposal to introduce the course was developed twice but rejected each time by the superintendent's office.

Textbook Choice

Given the importance of textbooks in determining what students are taught, the ability of teachers to select the textbook they use is another important element in influencing curriculum. Similar to district-wide curriculum development committees, district-wide textbook adoption committees were an important vehicle for teacher input in smaller districts.

Control over textbook selection has become a key issue for many school districts, and few schools in our survey gained much additional flexibility in textbook selection as a result of SBM. In the majority of districts, schools had to choose from among a limited number of texts adopted by the district, usually on the advice of a committee comprising of administrators and teachers. In some cases, districts adopted texts from a (similarly developed) state-sanctioned list. Texts for each subject were usually reviewed every three to five years.

❑ At an Adams County Twelve Five Star district high school, a SBM school, several mathematics teachers who wanted to change the textbook they used to teach calculus presented a proposal to the school's curriculum committee, which presented it to the school board. The board added the suggested textbook to the district-approved list, and it was ultimately adopted for use at the school.

The majority of schools in our sample did not change texts or the way texts were selected as a result of SBM. At the school level, the decision to select a particular text was most often made by consensus within departments with the concurrence of the principal, although principals retained veto power (but seldom exercised it). SBM's impact on text selection was to formalize the existing informal practice of giving teachers the responsibility of selecting texts from those on the state's and/or district's lists.

Textbook selection often hinged as heavily on budgetary considerations as on instructional issues. In several instances, however, SBM's budgetary flexibility allowed the purchase of class sets of books that would not have been possible otherwise. Some schools were severely hampered in textbook selection because of restrictive categorical funding arrangements.

Central office administrators raised several concerns about the implications of unrestricted textbook selection by schools. The first is an equity issue, particularly in districts with high student mobility. Supervisors were concerned that students moving from school to school, even within the same district, could have vastly different learning experiences if different texts were used in different schools. They also worried about how the lack of textbook standardization would affect results on district-wide examinations and state minimum competency tests. The second issue was the impact of text selection on the efforts of some districts to move away from a content- or text-based approach to a performance- or outcomes-based approach. According to supervisors, implementing NCTM standards might be difficult if schools were allowed to choose outside the approved list if schools attempted to redirect money elsewhere and keep old textbooks.

Other problems mentioned were comparability of evaluation and testing results across schools, adequacy of preparation of students for subsequent courses (especially in mathematics), difficulties integrating students who move from one school to another that covers different material, and the additional costs incurred in purchasing multiple texts (especially if only one teacher is using the text).

Changes in Instructional Practices

Instructional practices, loosely defined, refers to all the activities that teachers/schools do to implement the curriculum. Many national, state, and district reforms have been enacted that directly address the ways in which teachers attempt to engage students in learning. Rapid technological change also presents teachers with many more options for using technological developments.

Reforms, and indeed any innovative teaching practices, can and do occur in schools quite independently of SBM. The purpose of our study was not simply to catalogue innovative practices, but to determine the extent to which SBM had contributed to their implementation.

We found that in almost every school, teachers said that they already had considerable flexibility over their instructional/teaching methods. (This finding is not unique to this study.) However, SBM appears to be useful in creating an environment for change (e.g., by increasing teachers' feelings of professionalism and collegiality, by allowing schools to more appropriately target resources, and thus influence the pace of change). In the findings presented below, one caveat is necessary: although we found examples of SBM impacts on instruction in more than half of the schools in our sample, the overall impact has been small. A major exception occurred where teaching teams are in place, primarily in middle schools. Lacking an appropriate set of non-SBM comparison schools, we are unable to say with certainty whether the changes in instructional practices on teaching team situations were significantly different or encouraged by SBM.

The most widespread change in instructional practice encouraged by SBM was the introduction of a broader range of teaching styles, including cooperative learning, small group discussions and tutorials, an increased focus on problem solving and research courses, greater use of manipulatives in mathematics classes, and more hands-on lessons and real-world applications. These are all consistent with the changes suggested in the NCTM standards.

❑ Two schools in New Mexico used SBM procedures to opt into the Re:Learning model, which reinforced the use of all of the above teaching practices.

❑ A Salt Lake City high school used a discovery learning model to teach eighth-grade science. Students were given the state's objectives at the beginning of the course and asked to decide how they could reach them, what projects and research they would need to do, how they would report on their progress, and how they should be graded. Several schools also began using different assessment techniques, such as buddy exams and portfolio assessments to complement these new teaching styles.

SBM contributed to changing instructional patterns by allowing teachers increased access to professional development (e.g., one school bought each mathematics teacher a copy of the NCTM standards), by allowing resources to be allocated (e.g., for purchase of manipulatives), but perhaps most importantly, by changing attitudes within schools and the district. We were told in some schools, for example, that (as to be expected) teachers were more likely to use equipment they had ordered for themselves than when it was supplied to them. Teachers in one school resisted using "thousands of dollars'" worth of manipulatives that the district had supplied to each mathematics class because, they complained, they had not been trained how to use them.

Scheduling Flexibility. Some schools used the SBM process to make significant changes to the school timetable to accommodate instructional changes. Five high schools adopted some form of block scheduling, which allowed trade-offs of time between subjects, such as by using double-period lab classes. This flexibility is particularly important in science classes where the teacher has had to set up materials for the students. One teacher said, "Students don't get to learn nearly as much as when they do it for themselves."

Four high schools adopted teaching team arrangements similar to the approach common in middle schools. Typically, teaming in high schools operated in only one or two grades, or in school-within-school programs. Teams usually consisted of the teachers of the "core" subjects (English, mathematics, science, and social studies). Each team was assigned about 100 to 120 students. Students were usually taught each subject each day (plus electives). Each teacher had one individual planning period and a common planning period with the other teachers in the team. Teachers said that they primarily used these joint planning periods to address students with special needs and attitude and behavior problems. They could also use the planning period to design collaborative, integrative subject matter. The teams were also free to alter the time within their "block" for a particular lesson by mutual consent.

Integrating Material. More than half of the schools observed integrated material covered in two or more courses.

❑ In a Prince George's County high school, English teachers asked students to write a biography of a mathematician. A social studies teacher incorporated map reading, use of coordinates, and some graph reading at the same time these topics were being covered in mathematics class.

❑ At an Albuquerque middle school, the mathematics teachers gave their mathematics vocabulary list to the language arts teacher so that the vocabulary was also taught in language arts classes that week.

❑ Two Salt Lake City high school science teachers taught a biochemistry unit by combining chemistry and biology classes. One teacher was thus freed up for additional course preparation, and everyone benefited from the exchange of ideas. Also, the science teachers collaborated with mathematics teachers to incorporate mathematics concepts in chemistry. The reinforcement resulted in better prepared chemistry students.

Thematic units, where each class worked on a particular aspect of a larger project, were also popular. SBM institutionalized such efforts in some schools.

❑ Several teachers at an Adams County Twelve Five Star district high school conducted research on interdisciplinary teaching methods, developed a structure for it in their particular school, and discussed it with the principal. The issue was then presented to the curriculum committee and adopted for use in the school. This teaching method encompassed both block/alternative scheduling and subject integration, and placed heavy emphasis on project-oriented instruction and cooperative learning. The curriculum was based on thematic units (e.g., Patterns, Change, Diversity, and Interdependence); within each unit, students studied topics across the four disciplines (English, mathematics, science, social studies) in the core program.

❑ A Santa Fe middle school developed an interdisciplinary unit with science as the theme. The unit revolved around a "contraption symposium" (a takeoff on science fairs). Each student had to invent a "contraption," make a model of it, make an oral presentation, do "market research" (generate and interpret data and use charts and graphs), and develop advertising for it.

Expanded/Faster Introduction of New Technology. The role of SBM was most obvious in increasing the level and usage of technology in mathematics and science teaching, a result of the increased budget flexibility inherent in SBM. For example, while many of the schools already used graphing calculators, computers, laser disks, video microscopes, and overhead projection calculators to one extent or another, about half the schools reported that SBM budgeting procedures allowed them to either purchase more equipment (such as whole-class sets of calculators) or more extensive and appropriate software. Most often, these equipment purchases originated as requests from within a department and were subsequently approved by the site council (such as the construction of the computer lab at a Fort Worth middle school and the purchase of an Algebra Item Bank by the mathematics department of a Dade County high school).

❑ At a Bellevue middle school, the greatest impact on instructional methods arose from the technology program. (This program was funded separately from the SBM program, and was a district-wide activity. However, each school decided how to implement the program and spend its money. The SBM process gave teachers considerable flexibility in using these funds.) In some classrooms, teachers changed their role from lecturer/presenter to facilitator/coordinator of student learning. For example, students worked at computers and then came back to the group and shared what they had learned, thus becoming more involved in their own learning. According to the principal, this program was a good example of how the local decision-making process can work when money is available to support it. "Technology is supposed to thread throughout the curriculum, it is not just bringing in hardware and hoping that it works. To do this well, teachers also need in-service in how to make it [technology] more useful in the classroom."

In the schools we visited, we were given many other examples of how SBM had given teachers—either individually or as departments or interdisciplinary teams—the freedom to try new things or the money to implement them, such as:

❑ Funding field trips, excursions, and in-school performances.

❑ Establishing cooperative programs between high schools and their feeder schools, and with universities, vocational and community colleges, and night schools.

❑ Establishing business/industry links or making greater use of volunteers or consultants.

❑ Instituting systematic mechanisms for recognizing and rewarding students for academic performance and behavior.

While these practices are not radically innovative, they are helpful and inexpensive, and were being instigated by the schools themselves as responses to their own recognized needs. All were credited with helping to create positive environments and raising staff morale.

Some Overall Observations on SBM Effects on Instructional Practices. SBM encouraged the examples of changes in instructional practice noted above. The changes appeared to be beneficial in and of themselves. While many of the innovations occurred in isolation, some of the most promising examples were part of broader, whole-school development, as the following example from a Prince William middle school illustrates.

❑ In the past, all middle schools in the district used the same curriculum, and the same texts. Under SBM, diversity between schools grew, as did greater use of supplementary and alternative texts.

The existing district-wide instructional process model did not change with the introduction of SBM. However, to inform the teachers about differences in learning styles in their students, the principal of one middle school bought National Association of Secondary School Principals (NASSP) mate-

rials with school-managed funds. These materials had implications for how students are grouped, etc. which will impact instructional practices in the future.

The school also used school funds to offer professional development and in-service opportunities for teachers, which enabled them to make further changes in instruction. The science department head who attended a summer school program about cooperative learning and integration of science/mathematics/technology education shared the information with other teachers in the school. For example, since lasers were becoming more important in the Technology Education course, the science department instituted complementary teaching about lasers in the physics curriculum.

The science department chair at the school noted that teaching methods in the department were moving away from mostly lectures and lab demonstrations. With the additional resources available under SBM, teachers took advantage of other teaching tools, such as computers, video disks, and video microscopes. For example, faculty used a satellite dish to download NASA programs into the classrooms (e.g., on robotics and geology topics). One faculty member remarked, "This is like taking students on a field trip without having to pay for it, exposing students to ideas the faculty could not have done otherwise." The science department also made plans to network with other schools and counties.

Site-based decision making and funding at this school also allowed greater and more varied use of computers in the classrooms, which were linked to a file server in the library. All students in a class could thus work on the same program or on individual programs. This practice was not common in non-SBM schools in the county. The school also decided to hold a computer lab for each grade level, with 25 computers each, so that a whole class could have access at one time. To fund this class, money was taken from various allotments, the faculty gave up field trips for a few years, and some of the money saved on utilities accounts in the pilot years was used.

Danger of Introducing Too Many Innovations

Although one of the primary reasons for adopting SBM is to enable schools to innovate, the adoption of too many innovations simultaneously can create a situation where too little attention is paid to any one of them and undue stress is placed on school staff, the aggregate effect of the changes is actually detrimental to the school's SBM effort!

Though only a few of the school personnel we interviewed identified "doing too much" as a problem, others brought this issue up when asked about suggestions they would make to *other* schools.

❏ The mathematics department head at one middle school that was becoming a Re:Learning school as well as participating in the district's SBM effort noted that all the changes going on were sometimes distracting or overwhelming. He thought it might be useful to sometimes "step back and take a look at what they're doing."

❏ The principal of a middle school in another district cautioned against "project-itis," which he equated to seeking "quick fixes" to many school problems. He felt that school districts tended to adopt new projects haphazardly—"One year it's goals, the next it's strategic planning, and so on"—and expected the schools to shift their focus to the current project even when prior efforts still were ongoing. He noted that SBM needs a clear and consistent focus over an extended period of time to work.

❏ A group of science and mathematics teachers at one high school cautioned against "jumping in too fast, or trying to do everything at once." They also pointed out that teachers and departments often seemed to introduce a variety of "new things" at about the same time—e.g., new equipment, new software, new classes, interdisciplinary teaching. This onslaught can overload the teachers involved.

❏ A group of science and mathematics teachers serving on a district-level curriculum team in another community similarly noted that teachers were often asked to introduce or adapt to many changes at the same time. For example, at the same time they were making changes to the content of one or more courses at the direction of the district or state, or because of textbook changes, they were being asked to also make SBM-related changes. This problem was compounded for teachers who taught a variety of subjects since they could be dealing with changes in several subject areas at the same time.

We note that decentralization is particularly compatible with or even expected for certain kinds of changes, such as when schools are adopting teaching teams or instructional approaches such as "Re:Learning schools" (which use teaching teams). Thus, adding SBM or other related forms of decentralization should be less of a burden.

RECOMMENDATIONS

1. School districts should pilot new techniques that involve substantial cost and other risks in one school, evaluate the pilot, and quickly disseminate the findings to other schools. When ideas originate within one school the district should encourage systematic evaluations of the innovations by the school, so that other schools can learn from the experience, even if the trial is not successful. Evaluations should identify strengths and weaknesses, do's and don'ts, and the dollar cost and staff time required to learn how to use the new instructional practice.

2. School districts should allow faculty more input into choice of curriculum and textbooks to take advantage of the abilities and interests of science and mathematics faculty. The

district and individual schools should assess student interest in new elective courses in advance, perhaps determined by advance sign-up, as is done in Prince William County's high school.

3. Principals and site councils should explore ways to use SBM to encourage individual teachers to learn about and try out new instructional practices. For example, allocate funds and make time available for in-service training to inform teachers about new approaches, or encourage external suppliers to provide accessible briefings to faculty. These efforts should be coordinated with central-level science and mathematics personnel, who, as we previously recommended, should seek out new science and mathematics instructional approaches (both procedural and equipment-based), evaluate them, and to bring those approaches with potential to the attention of school faculty, perhaps by helping arrange vendor visits to schools.

4. After a new instructional technique has been tested and adopted by one or more faculty members, school districts, and individual schools should encourage those faculty to inform other faculty about the technique, and tactfully provide learning opportunities to these other faculty members. In general, other faculty should not be pressured to conform to the new practices but should be given ample opportunities to learn about and experiment with them.

5. Schools participating in SBM, and the groups with decision-making authority or advisory capacity, such as site councils and science and mathematics departments, should watch for innovation overload in SBM schools and limit the amount of change going on at any one time. Site councils or departments might consider keeping some kind of record of the number and types of changes that are already affecting teachers and department heads so that they can assess the impact of additional changes. Similarly, school districts should avoid asking or requiring schools to adopt major multiple changes at the same time. Districts should also

keep a record of the changes imposed on schools from various sources and review it when considering additional changes.

6. Schools, or school districts, should consider delaying introduction of SBM if the school is already engaged in a considerable amount of change. The determination should be based on the magnitude and types of changes already under way.

CHAPTER 14

SBM Effects on Students

One of the main arguments for introducing SBM is to give teachers and schools the tools to improve the performance of students (particularly in mathematics and science). Freeing schools and their faculty from rigid central control and school bureaucracy is supposed to unleash the creative potential of teachers to strengthen their teaching practices and address the particular needs of their students in ways that far-off administrators cannot. It would seem reasonable that self-managed schools would lead to significantly improved outcomes for students.

As noted in the introduction to this report, this study focuses on the *processes* of SBM and its effects on mathematics and science education rather than student learning *outcomes*. The design of this study means that we cannot with confidence attribute causality to findings on student outcomes. (Even if pre- and post-intervention measures for SBM and non-SBM had been available, it would still have been very difficult to extract SBM effects from the uncontrolled influence of other contemporaneous and interrelated reform efforts, such as external social and economic factors, increased state and district accountability requirements, the growth of the middle school philosophy and team teaching, the effective-schools movement, and the widespread influence of the development of national standards for mathematics. Also, time is a factor since changes in student performance often lag behind reform efforts considerably. Finally, the introduction of SBM is seldom a single event; it is typically a series of sometimes partial and fragmented delegations of authority. For all of these reasons, attribution of changes in student performance to the generic concept of SBM and decentralization requires caution.

We, however, asked teachers, department chairs, principals, and central office personnel their *perceptions* of SBM's effect on:

- Mathematics and science grades.
- Mathematics and science standardized achievement tests.
- Interest and motivation in science.
- Interest and participation in mathematics and science extracurricular activities.
- Interest in pursuing mathematics and science careers.

FINDINGS

The most common reaction of respondents at all levels was to disclaim knowledge of SBM impacts on student learning. This issue did not appear to be a high priority for the majority of those interviewed, and few school districts and schools had undertaken systematic assessments of the effects of SBM. There seemed to be no differences between districts based on the length of time they had been engaged in SBM.

Many schools, however, cited indications of greater student *interest* in science and mathematics education, due at least in part to SBM.

District-Level Views

The lack of awareness of student outcomes was most prominent at the central level and cut across all districts. A few central office personnel voiced our own concerns about attributing causality, given the other reforms also operating in their districts. One administrator responded, "Why would you expect it [SBM] to have any effect? That's not what SBM is about." Another said, "It will take 13 years [presumably the time for a child to pass completely through the system] for SBM to have any significant effect."

Still others responded that the types of learning encouraged by SBM are not necessarily the skills measured by standardized tests, and that other types of outcome measures (not yet taken) would be needed to draw appropriate conclusions. But the majority of those interviewed at the central level either expressed no view, or postulated that student test scores or grades had or should have improved, without firm evidence.

This lack of knowledge of mid-level district staff on SBM impacts suggests certain conclusions:

❑ In implementing SBM, districts have not given high priority to developing a vision of what SBM is ultimately supposed to achieve for students. If such views were articulated by superintendents and boards, they were not adequately communicated within the district administration and certainly not internalized.

❑ In implementing SBM, central district personnel were primarily concerned with processes rather than outcomes. This is not surprising, because districts have a definable impact on processes. This concern for processes was also evident in the roles that district personnel played in monitoring the introduction of SBM. Typically, they were most concerned with each school's adherence to union contracts, state and district board policies, and financial regulations, and with problems in implementation, such as disputes over decision making. They were not as interested in determining whether any of the newly given powers had been used to achieve anything substantive. Few districts performed evaluations of the outcomes of implementing SBM (those available to us focused mostly on processes). If any such studies exist, their results do not appear to be widely known by central personnel.

School-Level Views

At the school level, the picture is somewhat brighter. About half the schools in our sample identified some positive outcomes for students deriving from some school-based decision (a broader definition than school-based decision making). Of these, respondents in six schools related anecdotal evidence of improvements but could not provide convincing documentation. Six other schools merely indicated that they suspected improvements had occurred. In 7 of the 19 schools, the majority of respondents did not believe there had been any impacts on students or did not have an opinion. None of the schools, however, reported negative impacts for students. (Grades in one school had declined in recent years, but school personnel attributed this to factors external to the school.)

Within each school different staff had different perceptions of outcomes (perhaps reflecting differences in access to information); principals asserted positive changes more often than department heads or teachers.

While the effects of SBM become apparent only over time, we observed no general trends in the effectiveness of schools with different lengths of SBM experience. Some of the schools that had changed educational practices had been self-managing for only short amounts of time, while some operating under some form of SBM for several years still showed no evidence of change. Nor was there any consistent trend between the extent of decentralization of budgetary, staffing, or curriculum powers and significant gains in achievement. Some schools with relatively little added responsibility and authority achieved dramatic results, as had others with extensive autonomy. On the other hand, some schools with significant delegation of responsibility and a record of real changes in the delivery of instruction appeared to have achieved little gain.

■ *CHANGES IN STUDENT GRADES AND STANDARDIZED TEST RESULTS*

We queried respondents on any SBM-related effects on student science and mathematics grades, including Advanced Placement (AP) scores or standardized test results. While many schools were required to test some grades annually in mathematics, only a few districts had annual science testing programs.

❑ In one high school, none of the faculty interviewed claimed that grades had improved since the introduction of SBM. Some teachers felt that student interest and motivation had improved, which would ultimately affect grades. The department head anticipated that student grades in a new, teacher-developed course, "Science in Today's World," would be higher and that students would have a better comprehension of scientific principles. (This course is more "hands on" and less theoretical than other courses and is aimed at the middle-lower end of the ability range). No change in standardized test results was noted.

❑ In a high school in another district, no one interviewed was aware of improvement in science and mathematics grades. Most school personnel responded that they either did not know if there had been any changes in test scores or that there was no discernible change. One science teacher reported that SAT scores had risen by 10 points over the last few years but was extremely cautious about linking this to any one factor.

Neither mathematics teacher reported any discernible changes in SAT scores.

❑ There did appear to be positive changes at a Dade County high school, mostly due to improvements in student attendance, attitude, and discipline (discussed below). The school developed specific programs targeted at particular groups of students, which it termed successful. Summer schools, funded and organized through the SBM process, were used for advancement as well as make-up, which was credited with promoting higher enrollments in AP courses and increases in AP scores. Graduation rates and grades had been increased for at-risk students after this school created a school-within-a-school, which allowed a team of teachers to focus intensively on this small group of students.

❑ Science teachers interviewed in a Dade County middle school thought that working in teams would improve science performance but had no confirming data. There was no standardized test of science across the district.

❑ At a Prince William County middle school, grades improved for students in the summer school program (based on figures cited in the school plan), and to a lesser extent for those in the after-school programs (because of more homework completed, secure environment, etc.). All but one student who attended the summer school received a passing grade the next semester. The principal thought that it was too early to tell whether there was an effect on student achievement but thought it likely.

❑ The principal and several teachers of a Salt Lake City high school provided anecdotal evidence that the changes in school environment had indirectly improved student performance in mathematics and science. This relationship was hard to demonstrate because test scores had always been fairly high (on average). However, they believed that interest and performance at the top end of the ability range had increased, particularly in science. Most science and mathematics teachers saw improvements in grades and in participation in such programs as Honors programs and International Baccalaureate but did not know how much of this could be attributed to SBM. Five years ago, the school was considered to be very poor academically. Now it is highly ranked in such competitions as the state science competition, academic decathlon, etc. Further, the school credited the achievement at the top end with having a trickle-down effect on the bottom group of students. SBM was considered responsible, at least in part, for increasing the help the school gave outstanding students, such as giving them opportunities for outside experiences (university extension programs, etc.).

❑ Teachers at a Hillsborough junior high school said that achievement and test results had improved for students in this school-within-a-school program. Regular students also improved because SBM-inspired activities improved classroom discipline, allowing teachers to concentrate on teaching and reducing student distractions. Performance in mathematics was least improved.

❑ Neither the principal nor the teachers of a Prince William County high school could generalize about increases in grades because of SBM, and no study had yet been done to determine impacts. This school had always had high levels of achievement, but was changing demographically. However, some teachers pointed to specific areas of improvement resulting from school-initiated programs. The availability of additional equipment acquired because of SBM (graphing calculators, computers, and overhead projecting calculators) was credited with raising the AP scores. Tutorials for Spanish-speaking students and SAT preparation classes had been initiated but had not produced any impact yet.

❑ The principal of a Salt Lake City intermediate school believed that changes in his intermediate school, such as the tighter supervision of teachers, indirectly produced improvements in student performance in mathematics and science. (However, many of these changes were made at the direction of the principal rather than the site council.) Some teachers felt that student performance had probably increased because of the programs they were able to introduce with SBM funding. They cited evidence that more students were completing homework and fewer were getting grades of "Incomplete." However, the school's "failure-free" policy distorts this analysis. Any student with a grade below C- received an Incomplete or No Grade, usually for non-attendance, or a P, meaning working to capacity but not expected to pass. Students with an Incomplete had to attend an eighth period (after school) and summer school for remediation (funded through flexible use of funds). Another innovation introduced by the school was a trimester system (allowed by the state on a trial basis). Test scores following the change to trimesters improved an average of 13 points. The principal attributed some of the improvement to the availability of more electives and greater teacher efficiency because teachers had to cover the material more quickly.

❏ Most of those interviewed in one Fort Worth middle school thought that the efforts of the school (although not necessarily SBM) had a positive impact on student achievement and interest in mathematics and science. However, the adoption of the middle-school approach (a district-wide policy) at about the same time as the initial SBM effort had more impact. The principal said that grades had increased while end-of-year failures had decreased. The additional instructors hired by the school under SBM addressed student deficits recognized by the faculty, not only in academics but in self-esteem. Students were started in algebra in the eighth grade, a significant change from the past, and some classes in lower grades were taught some algebraic concepts. SBM decisions also facilitated tutoring in mathematics and science.

❏ According to the principal of one Hillsborough high school, students at the upper levels who had taken advantage of the new opportunities available under SBM had made considerable gains. These students had been very successful in state competitions and AP calculus exams. The principal attributed most of the student improvement to the change in relationships among teachers through the reassignment of faculty duties, the tutorial program, and the change in philosophy.

Many schools had school goals, mission statements, or School Improvement Plans. But, in general, we did not find that the schools linked these or their expressed objectives (such as improved student interest and learning) directly to school operations—for example, by: a) relating budgets to objectives; b) asking for significant new mathematics and science proposals to be related to mathematics and science department objectives; or c) explicitly tracking achievement of these objectives.

■ *STUDENT INTEREST, MOTIVATION, ELECTIVES SELECTION, AND PARTICIPATION IN EXTRACURRICULAR ACTIVITIES*

We asked school administrators and science and mathematics faculty for their perceptions of changes in student attitudes, behavior, interest, and motivation related to mathematics and science, and about any increases in enrollment in elective classes, or student participation in mathematics- or science-related extracurricular activities, such as math clubs, science fairs, and summer schools.

In contrast to academic improvements, the majority of persons interviewed reported significant increases in student interest and motivation in mathematics and science attributed to specific programs established as a result of school-centered decision making. Positive changes were reported by 15 of the 19 schools. However, many of the changes in the middle schools were associated with teaching teams. While such teaming entails a major element of delegation to faculty, most educators probably would not equate teaming with SBM. Also, these perceptions are anecdotal for the most part. Nevertheless, teaching teams do represent an important form of decentralization, closely related to SBM.

❏ The principal of a Santa Fe middle school reported that student interest rose with the number of teachers trained to use different delivery methods and engage students more. His evidence consisted of students' statements to him and the quality of their portfolios. A science teacher believed that some students were more involved because of cooperative learning. A mathematics teacher reported an increase in student interest and motivation, based on student requests to be in the advanced part of the class. Another mathematics teacher noted several signs of interest: students were taking more ownership of their work; students were viewing teachers as coaches rather than instructors; and students appeared to have better comprehension of subject areas as a result of additional attention resulting from teaching "families," smaller classes, and curriculum integration.

❏ One Albuquerque high school teacher said that the greatest change due to SBM was more student interest and motivation. A small increase occurred in the number of students interested in participating in extracurricular activities, such as the Los Alamos think tank, a summer science program held at the Los Alamos Laboratories.

❏ Both mathematics and science teachers at an Adams County Twelve Five Star district high school reported noticeable changes in student interest and participation in extracurricular activities. For example, 50 students signed up for the Nature Guide Program and Woodlands project, an exceptional number.

❏ Average attendance at a Prince George's County high school increased from 85 percent to 90 percent, primarily in grades nine and ten (where team teaching had been introduced), but also to a lesser extent in later grades (presumably among students who progressed into those grades from the team teaching environment). The science teachers reported that the number of students in AP science courses increased from 22 to 66 over the last two years, which they attributed to greater encouragement from the team approach.

❑ The principal of a Kalispell high school noted that more students were participating in programs sponsored by the university and were spending more of their free time working in the computer lab. He also cited the good support for a recently sponsored math fair, which was exceptionally well attended by students (more than 300). The mathematics department head indicated that more students were enrolling in the college preparation program.

❑ The principal of a Prince George's County middle school reported that enrollment in higher level courses (pre-algebra and algebra) increased while enrollment in general math decreased. The principal related this shift to the School Improvement Plan focus on opportunities to learn. When teachers felt that seventh-graders were ready to take pre-algebra, the school modified the county guideline to facilitate the change. Instead of requiring the students to meet all guideline criteria for taking pre-algebra, including a teacher's recommendation, a grade of B or better in sixth grade, and a certain score on the county criterion reference test, the school ruled that students who met one of these criteria could take pre-algebra.

❑ As a result of school-initiated programs, including tutoring and teaming, the faculty in a Fort Worth middle school reported that students felt teachers cared about them personally. School actions to increase participation in school activities, such as science fairs, essay writing, and math competitions, improved students' self-esteem as well as academic performance.

❑ The major outcome due to SBM in a Dade County high school was increased attendance. Graduation rates were also higher than prior to SBM. Enrollments increased in AP courses and in calculus and trigonometry classes, which was attributed to extra skills students gained in summer school classes, stimulated by the SBM activity. Math club membership increased to 80 participants. Faculty sponsors of extracurricular clubs were paid, which was not possible before SBM. SBM allowed the creation of clubs not covered by the existing contract.

❑ At this same Dade County high school, one SBM outcome was the development of a school-within-a-school for eleventh-graders who were at risk of not graduating. A team of teachers was assigned to teach a daily four-hour block of English, math, science, and social studies, allowing greater flexibility in presenting course material. The program increased attendance and brought students who had dropped out back to school. Much of the success of the program came from setting high expectations for students.

❑ A Prince William County middle school science department head said that SBM had a positive impact on students' interest and enjoyment of science because the classes were now more "hands on," not just lectures. "Students are more involved and using more equipment. They are learning more because they are doing more." Test scores didn't show improvement for all students, but she expected them to do so in the future because students now had more opportunities for new activities than before. Student interest in the science fair and ecology and science clubs increased, partly because SBM provided the flexibility to use school funds for school transport.

❑ A major impact of SBM reported by the teachers and principal of a Dade County middle school was an increase in attendance. Discipline also improved. The principal remarked, "Kids know that something will be done if they misbehave. Improving behavior outside the classroom has led to better classroom behavior. This more than anything has improved morale for students and teachers." The focus on discipline developed from faculty recommendations emerging from SBM processes.

❑ A Salt Lake City high school reported much greater participation in extracurricular activities and competitions under SBM. Increased achievement at the top end also caused a trickle-down effect for the bottom group of students.

❑ Student attitudes and motivation increased at a Salt Lake City intermediate school through Parent-Link, an automated telephone system purchased through the flexible use of school funds. This system gave more responsibility to parents for their children's performance, but not all parents took advantage of it. SBM led to the generation of considerable school pride, which was a priority of the school community council, and which fed back to the students and the community.

■ *EFFECTS ON MINORITY AND FEMALE STUDENTS*

We also asked respondents whether there had been any special SBM effects on science and mathematics education for minority or female students. No differences or effects were noted in 10 of the 19 schools. However, some of these schools had high minority enrollments, and the positive outcomes of SBM for students in general also applied to them. In a few schools, the number of females enrolling in mathematics and science elective courses increased (although only to a small extent), but usually there was no clear evidence that SBM played a significant role.

❑ One Adams County Twelve Five Star district high school could not identify any differential performance for minorities (minority enrollment less than 2 percent), but more females were reported to have enrolled in science courses over the past few years (unspecified in number), and 40 percent of the organic chemistry class was female.

❑ An Albuquerque high school was part of a state "Gender Equity Project" to heighten sensitivity to gender equity issues. Most teachers did not detect any impacts on females as a result of SBM, except for an (unspecified) increase in enrollment in computer and chemistry classes.

❑ In a Prince William County middle school, a higher proportion of students from minority groups was able to attend the summer school and after-school programs developed through

SBM-related efforts because school funds could be used to support these programs.

❑ The Hillsborough middle school's school-within-a-school program helped at-risk students, many of whom were minorities. The program provided positive role models by using minority teachers. Female students in the program showed improved attitudes because they were challenged more by being required to do pre-algebra.

❑ A Prince William County high school's plan addressed specific needs of disadvantaged students by providing twice-weekly after-school lessons, tutorials, and transportation for these students. At the request of students, parents, and faculty, the school also held extra SAT preparation classes for disadvantaged students, using SBM funds to pay the instructors. Through ESL and tutorials, students felt more comfortable in asking questions and enrolling in higher level courses. SAT scores increased for students in the tutorial program.

❑ The same high school used teaching teams, also a result of SBM, which produced positive effects on minority and female students. Such teams accomplished much more work, allowed teachers to work faster than before, encouraged students to be grouped heterogeneously and to work together, and increased self-esteem. Students came to know each other better. More female students took higher level mathematics courses. A plan for increasing the performance of female students in AP physics was included in the budget.

RECOMMENDATIONS

District Level

1. Greater attention needs to be given by central administrators, including the mathematics and science specialists, to

articulating to the schools the ultimate impacts of SBM on students. Reinforce the concept that SBM is a tool rather than an end in itself.

2. District evaluation and monitoring plans should have a greater focus on outcomes, and findings should be communicated to all. Circulate specific examples of successful practices.

School Level

3. Each school should develop a "vision" of what the school wants to accomplish and communicate this to the departments and faculty. The vision should address the objectives of the SBM/decentralization approach and its ultimate purpose of improving student interest and achievement. The science and mathematics departments should also articulate their own vision for encouraging student interest and achievement and indicate how success could be measured in science and mathematics.

4. Individual schools should perform impact evaluations of significant changes/innovations the school introduces, such as significant new teaching equipment, software, or new teaching approaches. Include estimates of the effects of the changes on student interest/attitudes/motivation towards science and mathematics subject matter, including changes in enrollments in electives and extracurricular activities. The science and mathematics departments should attempt to assess the effects of change on actual learning achievement based on grades and test scores, and surveys of students and parents. Additionally, the evaluations should break out outcomes for categories of students, such as by minority status and gender, to identify educational approaches that may be particularly helpful for these students.

5. The math and science faculty should attempt to make evaluations of learning as robust as possible (e.g., by using

accepted experimental and control procedures) but should also include qualitative analysis where necessary (such as systematically obtained ratings from affected students).

6. Schools should annually survey faculty for feedback on changes resulting from increased school, department, and teacher flexibility, and for suggestions on improving the decentralization process. Faculty should be asked about student outcomes as well as their own morale and feelings of accomplishment in educating students. Segregate findings by department so that departments such as mathematics and science can identify what has occurred in their own areas. (A school might choose not to disseminate department findings outside the individual department.)

7. Schools should require departments to link proposals for new activities, both budgeting and nonbudgeting actions, to school goals and objectives that relate to student interest and achievement, probably through written justification material. If the school as a whole does not do this, science and mathematics departments should internally incorporate such linkages into their own educational decisions.

PART THREE

Overall Findings and Recommendations

CHAPTER 15

Suggestions by SBM Practitioners

At the conclusion of each interview, we asked respondents for their recommendations to other schools or school districts interested in starting or improving an SBM program, particularly as it affected mathematics and science. Their responses give a good indication of the issues uppermost in the minds of those with experience in SBM. Most, but not all, of the suggestions made by the participants are reflected in the earlier chapters of this report.

Suggestions by school-level personnel (teachers and principals) are presented first, followed by those of district-level personnel. Responses in the two groups were quite similar.

While we asked for suggestions about how other schools and school districts could use SBM to improve math and science, most responses were not specific to these subjects. As one science department head said, "If SBM is not working in general, it is not likely to work for any subject in particular. Improvements in math and science come about as a by-product of the process that comes about from the freeing up of ideas."

Comments specifically concerning mathematics and science tended to be warnings about the limitations of SBM: "One of the problems is the sequencing in math, which many teachers see as inhibiting experimentation." Similarly in another district, almost every person interviewed mentioned concerns for equity in a highly mobile student population—that is, if each school takes advantage of the flexibility of SBM to develop its own curriculum, there will be little continuity between different schools and different levels of schooling in the same district.

SUGGESTIONS

From School-Level Personnel

Some respondents used this opportunity to make general observations about their experiences rather than specific suggestions. For example, one principal said, "It [SBM] is nothing to fear. It is not an erosion of power. It makes coming to school enjoyable because you don't have to carry the burden of all the school's problems yourself."

We have grouped the suggestions by the topics addressed most frequently: a) training needs; b) amount of delegation; c) time and incentives needed; d) teacher involvement; e) need for voluntary participation; f) role of the principal; g) communication; and h) need to share information among schools.

Training Needs. The most frequently offered suggestion concerned the need for adequate training for participants in SBM, with specific training in decision-making techniques, budgeting, and team building, as well as the need for everyone within the school to be trained. Typical suggestions were:

"Intensive start-up training, focusing on collaborative management and consensus-building topics, should be provided to the full staff. Ongoing in-service training, specifically tailored to SBM topics, should also be provided."

"This training should focus on enhancing general management, time management, and business/finance/accounting skills. Many teachers are reluctant to assume budgeting/finance responsibilities because they feel they lack the proper knowledge, experience, and skills to make sound budget decisions."

"More emphasis needs to be placed on increasing the sense of professionalism among school staff; the faculty needs to feel capable of performing the responsibilities that they are delegated as a result of SBM."

Amount of Delegation. The second most frequent suggestion was that districts should delegate much more responsibility to schools than they do at present. Many teachers and principals felt frustrated by their very limited control over the budget, realizing that widespread change is not possible without the resources to implement it. Some recommended specific extra budget delegations that they believed would be beneficial, such as controlling the maintenance and utilities budget, and carrying over funds from year to year. Another common theme was the desirability of greater school control (or more specifically, principal control) over staffing decisions, particularly in firing unsatisfactory teachers, determining class sizes, and making teacher assignments.

Other recommendations were similar: "Districts should allow schools to be innovative;" "Districts should not put too many restrictions on schools;" and "Systems have to give strong signals to their administrators that support change, and be prepared to accept failure that will inevitably happen. Teacher unions also need to give support."

Even though many respondents recommended broader responsibilities for schools, many also suggested that schools start with SBM in only a few areas and expand as these efforts become successful. Some comments were:

> "SBM doesn't have to be totally in place when you start, but has to be sufficiently organized to make a good impression."

> "Don't leave it too open. Start slowly. Don't start with big things like budget and staffing. People have a hard time at first separating issues and personalities."

> "Don't jump into things too fast, don't try to do everything at once. Avoid change for change's sake. Be critical of what you are doing, and take a longer view."

Time and Incentives Needed. As well as starting small, several teachers warned that schools must allow sufficient time to elapse for SBM to succeed: "Do not expect real change for three years or more; you have to persevere and not let it die." Two principals recommended warnings: "Expect opposition. No one likes change. It takes time to adapt to change and the first year is going to be rough;" "Be sure to understand that they will go through some stress, and they need to be flexible;" "To really understand the concept, take one step at a time, see how it fits, see what changes people are willing to make. Network and learn from others. Realize that it involves a lot of experimentation, and that everything won't work out."

Personnel at the majority of sites visited strongly recommended that schools provide sufficient time, opportunity, and resources for the site council to give proper consideration to issues. Those experienced with SBM clearly regard effective time management as a critical element in the success of SBM:

> "SBM wears people out. It is not just time, but that the time is being used unproductively. Maybe better training and experience can overcome this. You have to make an attempt to minimize meetings, or at least make them shorter."

"Teachers are tired of being told thank you. They need greater rewards/compensation for involvement, either more time or more money."

"Provide incentives to make people want to be part of the SBM team, that it will make a difference to the school, and is not seen as just one more thing to do. Build it into the calendar—set aside quality time for it."

"Additional school time has to be given so that SBM meetings or SBM-related business can be conducted during the school day. Having to hold meetings during lunch breaks or in the afternoon (without additional pay) is a disincentive to teacher participation in SBM."

Sharing Decision Making with Teachers. Another common theme emerging from the suggestions of respondents was the need for principals to share power, and for the teachers to have input into decision making. Sometimes this concept was expressed as a need for building a sense of community or team building within the school. Others attributed the apparent success of SBM in their school to the practice of shared decision making already established in the district: "A spirit and practice of teamwork will have to be established and sustained through trust and communication between all participants."

In addition, 11 respondents suggested that schools should devise ways of including as many teachers as possible in decision making. A few schools suggested including parents and students also:

"Some mechanism to broaden teacher involvement is needed—perhaps soliciting a full faculty vote on more issues should be used."

"Be very open with teachers. Let them know that they are a valuable part of the process."

"SBM planning needs to focus more on how to involve teachers directly in the process, and some type of mechanism for keeping teachers continuously abreast of decisions that are made needs to be developed at the outset."

Voluntary Participation. While involving as many people as possible was strongly recommended, many of those queried warned that membership on the site council—and indeed, whether the school was involved in SBM at all—should be voluntary and involve only those with positive attitudes. Teachers in one school suggested that new staff should be hired only if they are supportive of and willing to be involved in SBM (i.e., willing to assume the additional responsibilities that are associated with SBM).

Role of the Principal. A number of interviewees emphasized that the principal has two key roles in ensuring the success of SBM: setting a vision of what SBM is trying to achieve, and exhibiting certain personal qualities. Comments directed toward the principal included:

> "Start with what it is that you want to achieve through SBM, and form your team according to this objective."

> "The principal has to have, and articulate, a vision of what the school is about."

> "You need to create a vision of the process before you start."

> "Have appropriate principals. SBM is only as good as the principal. If you have a weak principal, it will fail. In the implementation stage, you have to have meetings, but you also need someone to move it along. Some principals are overwhelmed—it happened to them too quickly. They were not trained well enough, especially in being business managers. The school system has to work out what to do with them. Good principals in the past do not necessarily make good SBM principals. Make sure principals are fair-minded and not dictatorial."

> "Administrators need to trust their staff, which means that scheduling, budgeting, and staffing have to be opened up. There has to be long-term commitment—SBM won't work if it is simply the latest response to a pattern and seen as a quick fix solution."

"As an administrator, be willing to let go of traditional
responsibilities, be honest, be willing to ask for teachers'
opinions. When the model is practiced from above, teachers will be willing to participate fully."

Communicating Responsibilities. Responses indicated that responsibilities must be clearly delineated, both within the school,
and between the school and the district: "It is essential that
schools clarify the roles and responsibilities that the various
school participants (principal, parents, site council, and subcom-
mittees) will assume at the beginning. This clarification of roles
is needed to avoid some of the conflicts that may arise between
the principal and other school decision-making bodies."

Sharing Information with Other Schools. The last common
theme to emerge from the suggestions of school-level respondents was the need to network and share information with other
schools and systems involved with SBM:

"Schools should send teachers/school staff to observe and
evaluate the SBM efforts of other schools prior to developing their own SBM program. This will allow them to
identify and avoid some of the problems that occur when
converting from a centralized to a decentralized system."

"Provide for sharing of information on innovations among
schools. Schools should be able to take advantage of the
experience of others. Department heads and faculty, for
example, might visit schools that are already doing some
major activity in which the school is interested."

From District-Level Personnel

Comments and suggestions offered by central-level personnel
interviewed did not differ substantially from those given by
teachers or principals. However, their comments reflected their
perspectives as administrators and were more often directed
toward districts than individual schools. These suggestions also

reflect concerns (often an undercurrent throughout the entire interview) about the security of their own positions under SBM.

We have grouped the district-level suggestions by the following topics: a) training needs; b) information about SBM; c) technology diffusion; d) working relations with school faculty; e) budgeting issues; and f) miscellaneous.

Training Needs. As with school-level respondents, those interviewed most often mentioned the need for adequate training of all participants—including district-level administrators. Some commented on the importance of training school principals as leaders: "Administrators—district and school—are the key. They have to see authority as something to be shared, they have to be ready for it."

Others commented on specific areas of perceived weaknesses, such as financial skills, team building and consensus building: "There is a need for a lot of training for teachers and parents involved in decision making—particularly related to budget and finance. Parents need education about curriculum. Training needs to be on-going because of the turnover of council members."

Information about SBM. Our respondents expressed the need for clarifying what SBM was supposed to be about—the district's vision of SBM and what role each level of the organization would play (similar to teachers' comments). As one administrator said, "Start with a mission statement and at least a skeleton of the policy towards SBM at the outset—we didn't have that up front, so there was a lot of confusion about what SBM meant. Some teachers thought that it meant they would be in control, so there was conflict between teachers and principals and a lot of suspicion and confusion, some of which still exists. A clearer picture would have helped—every one interpreted it [SBM] differently."

Technology Diffusion. Comments addressed the need for districts to carefully analyze the implications of SBM on central office technology-related functions: "Technology is one place where you can't decentralize completely. There needs to be a

central person who has the time and skills to evaluate the technical issues, to keep up with resources and innovation. This area is moving too fast for teachers to keep up with; what they need to focus on is what they want to do with technology, not the operational details."

Several mathematics and science supervisors also spoke of the legitimate need for a district office role in collecting and disseminating information about innovations in curriculum, teaching methods, and technology (such as the NCTM standards) at the state and national levels. As one science supervisor said, "Teachers do not have a monopoly on good ideas."

Central Staff Working Relations with School Faculty. Administrators understood that district personnel needed to change the way they related to school faculty under SBM, that they were evolving from directing and supervising teachers to a more consultative role. Comments by one central respondent and teachers in two schools in the district have a similar flavor:

> "There needs to be more of an effort at the central level to train supervisors and other central staff about their changing role to support SBM, instead of allowing it to become a source of fear or indifference. SBM won't work at the school level if it has to work in the same old environment."

> "What is needed are people who can be unbiased internal consultants, not mandators, who can help schools make decisions about what they can use and what the opportunities are."

> "There needs to be more of an attitude change—there is still so much coming down from above rather than bottom-up. A lot more training is needed for people at the middle management level in the county office. They are the most resistant to change. They don't stop it, but they do passively obstruct change."

Budgetary Issues. Budget directors often gave specific suggestions about decentralizing budget control which paralleled the suggestions offered by principals. Examples include:

> "Go for a single budget system, the same for all schools, otherwise it gets too difficult to do all of the projections. You need to establish detailed ground rules about what accounts have flexibility or not, what salaries can be converted, time lines, and so on."

> "Go at it slowly and carefully. Base the formula for allocating budget for staffing on the number of teachers rather than a dollar allocation. This prevents schools from playing games with people and positions. This provides a balance that is needed, and also provides an opportunity for the district to provide equitably for all students."

This theme of starting small—echoed by school personnel in a number of schools—was suggested by several central administrators. One recommended that districts "feel their way with how much latitude to give schools. Don't begin at the extremes, like here's your money, go spend it." Others recommended the more conventional and conservative approach of pilot studies ". . . to work out the kinks, to see how things work."

Some school personnel spoke of a need to budget using an average teacher salary to prevent schools from hiring the cheapest (and thus usually the most inexperienced) teachers.

Miscellaneous Suggestions. Many individuals interviewed made suggestions that could not be classified according to the topics identified above. These suggestions covered many broad areas, including establishing databases for needs analyses, focusing on the School Improvement Plan, improving in-school communication, and maintaining flexibility in making changes over time. In general, these miscellaneous suggestions were very similar to the recommendations drawn from our analyses in earlier chapters. However, one suggestion stands out as being particularly important: "Be open-minded, and don't be afraid to ask for help."

CHAPTER 16

Summary of Findings and Recommendations

This chapter provides highlights of our findings and recommendations from our examination of these 12 school districts and 19 schools. Detailed information is provided in previous chapters.

FINDINGS

We found little opposition in either the literature or in our own investigation of school districts to decentralization principles, such as the desirability of delegating responsibility to the level where learning activity takes place in order to encourage innovation, increase motivation, and ultimately, improve education for students.

Unfortunately, as so often happens, *implementation* of principles often falls far short of the ideal. SBM was implemented in markedly different ways in the districts we studied, none of them entailing delegation of powers as complete as that envisioned in the conceptual models. Thus, it can be argued that in schools that tried versions of SBM, "SBM" was not fully tested. Indeed, the question arises of whether a decentralization approach such as SBM *can be adequately implemented in the real world under current structural and financial school system conditions.*

Following are our key findings:

1. We found many noteworthy examples of small improvements in science and mathematics education. On the whole, the evidence suggests that science and mathematics teaching will improve if science and mathematics faculty are really allowed to share in decision making and have significant input into choices about educational practices. At the very least, real decentralization, such as SBM, is likely to enable these changes to occur sooner than otherwise. While the districts and schools seldom reported documented impacts of SBM on learning, many felt that student interest and involvement (in science and mathematics) had increased and would ultimately lead to increased learning.

2. The SBM efforts differed considerably with respect to allocation of authority, responsibility, and participation in decision making at the school, department, and classroom levels. There was no "cookie-cutter" approach across the country, or even within individual school districts.

3. Our findings confirm the contentions in the literature that schools have many substantial difficulties in SBM implementation. Often these problems were not overcome by the school system or the individual schools, and this was re-

flected in science and mathematics departments' experiences.

4. A common problem in the schools and districts we examined was confusion about roles and responsibilities under SBM. This lack of clarity affected all levels: the school, principal, site council, department heads, and individual science and mathematics faculty members. Science and mathematics faculty, including department heads, often were not clear as to what they could or could not do. (We ourselves were sometimes unable to put together a clear picture as to who could do what.)

5. Principals clearly played a key role in determining the success of SBM, especially whether departments and faculty took real advantage of SBM to make changes in their science and mathematics teaching. The extent to which the principal shared decision making and encouraged faculty to make suggestions was critical. Where faculty perceived that the principal was not truly delegating, teacher satisfaction and innovativeness decreased.

6. Probably the most frequent, substantive new delegation of responsibility by the school district to individual schools under SBM was greater control over their own budgets, including use of budgeted funds. This added responsibility appears to have been widely used by science and mathematics faculty in the schools we examined. The budget delegation usually translated to increased flexibility in the use of funds for supplies, equipment, professional development, substitute teachers, and the like. Basic personnel salaries and numbers of teachers, however, were still kept under tight central control. A small amount of leeway in personnel decisions occurred in a few cases where departments were able to trade off vacated faculty positions for other uses.

7. Within the schools, budgeting responsibility was usually further delegated to the department heads, who in turn

usually sought input from individual science and mathematics faculty members.

8. Science and mathematics *departments* often appeared to make good use of their increased responsibility and authority to request and obtain equipment and supplies; to undertake new teaching practices; to determine course content and sequence (within school district groundrules); and to influence the scheduling, format, and content of classes.

9. Some science and mathematics faculty also took advantage of their added flexibility to introduce new courses and alter course content and sequence. However, only a small proportion of the faculty made these changes. Most science and mathematics faculty seemed considerably more cautious in making changes, and often did not fully understand what new opportunities meant. The most beneficial change, according to science and mathematics *faculty*, was their greater capacity to obtain needed supplies and equipment.

Overall, the chief benefit that science and mathematics faculty derived from SBM can perhaps be best labelled as added *flexibility* to accomplish changes that they would not have been otherwise able to achieve, or only with a much greater expenditure of time and effort.

10. Science and mathematics faculty were often not convinced that site councils were doing a worthwhile job. This impression was due to the teachers' feeling that they lacked real representation on the council, lacked adequate feedback from the council, lacked a real opportunity to provide input to their council representatives, and lacked confidence that the principal was delegating real responsibility to the council (especially in schools where the principal often turned down council recommendations on major issues).

11. Inadequate communication among school administrators, staff, and the site council on SBM-related issues was a major problem frequently mentioned by science and mathe-

matics faculty. The uncertainty over what faculty could and could not do under SBM, the site council communication problems noted above, and the lack of regular faculty meetings on SBM-related issues, all contributed significantly to the faculty perceptions of "not being in the know."

12. Few schools gave adequate, if any, attention to evaluating their own efforts, especially the effects of activities on student learning and interest in science and mathematics. A small number of school districts (but no individual SBM schools) did survey students, parents, and staff. More of concern, however: none of the schools systematically assessed new teaching practices introduced by their faculty. Nor did the science and mathematics faculties. In part this may have been due to a failure of district and school administrators to establish and communicate a "vision" for the efforts aimed at improving student interest and learning.

13. By and large, little effort was expended within school districts to provide much communication *between* schools about SBM efforts or new teaching approaches tried in one (or more) other schools. Several science and mathematics faculties identified the desirability of such interchange.

14. While site councils play a major role in descriptive literature about SBM, they were not a very effective player in the schools we examined. The councils seldom focused on the large issues of curriculum or learning (science and mathematics or otherwise), such as how to improve student learning, reduce the school's drop-out rate, or how to improve testing. Schools that adopted specific learning-oriented reforms, such as "Re:Learning" schools, were more focused on educational improvement and used the flexibility provided by SBM in that area.

15. In most instances, parent and student involvement was not extensive, nor was it perceived by school personnel to have had substantial impact. Nevertheless, most school staff we interviewed believed it to be desirable. Most involvement

was as members of site councils and other SBM advisory committees. At most, only a small number of parents and students were involved in these efforts, raising questions about the extent to which they really represented all parents and all students—particularly if they were not elected.

16. Except for schools using teaching teams, only a few schools attempted to use their added flexibility to reach out to parents, especially parents of children with substantial school problems.

17. Science and mathematics teachers often complained about SBM but wanted more. Most approved of more input by faculty into school decisions but did not believe the system was working well, certainly not as well as it should.

RECOMMENDATIONS

As indicated in chapter 1, we did not attempt to systematically and quantitatively measure the impacts of SBM on students' interest in science and mathematics and their learning progress. Our findings on changes in teaching practices also suffer from lack of an evaluation design that provides strong evidence as to whether the added flexibility of SBM caused changes or the pace of change. Therefore, we have made recommendations only where we felt we had sufficient evidence from our interviews and examination of school materials to make informed judgments.

The recommendations presented in earlier chapters, highlighted here, are steps we believe school systems should try. If implemented, they may significantly alleviate many of the difficulties encountered in implementing SBM.

District Level

1. We recommend the continued application of school-based management approaches—that is, approaches that provide schools, departments, and faculty with real input into decisions about their own budgets, personnel issues, procurements, and instructional practices. Enough schools and their science and mathematics faculties had made achievements, though usually small, in science and mathematics education to warrant continued SBM effort.

2. SBM should be introduced into schools with principals who are able and willing to delegate responsibility. Provide new SBM principals with training and technical assistance in assuming a participatory facilitator/manager role rather than the traditional authoritarian role. Assist current principals in the transition to a SBM-type school by arranging for formal training and possibly mentoring.

3. The school district should provide a forum for the interchange of information among schools about new actions and new teaching approaches tried by individual schools. Include findings on the success of the new approaches, problems, and actions used to alleviate the problems. Place most of the responsibility for providing the information on individual schools and their departments, but have district science and mathematics specialists oversee this activity, assist the schools in preparing the information, and disseminate the information. A computerized network might help with this task.

4. Assign district-level science and mathematics specialists in a decentralized, SBM environment to take on the following important activities: a) provide information to science and mathematics faculties on faculty roles and responsibilities under SBM; b) disseminate information on new technologies (including evaluative information); c) provide information on training opportunities; d) provide technical assistance; e) encourage and help with evaluations of school innova-

tions or actually undertake them; and f) survey science and mathematics faculty periodically for ways to improve the usefulness of the *central* science and mathematics specialists' work.

School and District Level

5. A school district and each implementing school should clearly communicate the roles and responsibilities of the principal, department heads, and individual faculty under SBM. In the initial stages of implementation, the district and individual school may not have fully decided on appropriate roles. The areas of uncertainty should be made clear to all parties. After the trial implementation period (e.g., two years) the district and school should firm up and clarify groundrules. The roles and relationships of central and school personnel should be regularly reviewed. As school personnel gain more experience with their added decision-making roles, the extent of delegation might be increased.

6. Each school should work hard to provide adequate two-way communication among the principal, site council, department heads, and individual faculty members to encourage genuine participation in decision making. In addition to distributing minutes of site council meetings, schools should promote regular "feed-in" from department faculty members to their department heads, site council representatives, and each other. This input should be on both departmental matters (budget, department personnel, procurement, instructional matters) and school-wide issues (disciplinary matters, overall budgeting/expenditure, personnel issues). Regular department meetings should discuss opportunities for, and trials of, innovative science and mathematics education practices.

7. Delegation should not stop at the school level. It should be carried down through departments to individual faculty, giving them added flexibility such as in obtaining supplies

and equipment, participation in course scheduling and content, as well as instructional practices.

8. Faculty should not be forced into an "ideal" cooperative, interactive mold; SBM should not penalize individuality. Science and mathematics faculty will inevitably differ considerably in their personalities and preferences for teaching styles and practices. Give all faculty opportunities to participate in such activities as committees and the site council, but do not force such participation. Faculty that prefer to "work" by themselves can also benefit from SBM by utilizing the added flexibility that SBM provides to secure supplies and equipment and revise their instructional practices. These opportunities should be clearly communicated to them.

9. Schools should strongly encourage science and mathematics faculty to try new education approaches using the added flexibility of SBM. Tapping school ingenuity is probably the major potential advantage of a decentralized, SBM approach. The school and school district should include "innovating" explicitly in staff performance appraisals; give credit for trying new practices even if they are not always successful; and provide special recognition awards for successful innovations. (By innovations, we mean any practice that is new to the school, even if it is not new by national or district standards.)

10. School districts and individual schools should place considerably more emphasis on tracking changes in science and mathematics education practices and their impact on student outcomes (in terms of both student interest and achievement). The *quid pro quo* for giving more authority and responsibility to schools and their departments is more accountability for results. This step, however, will likely be most practical and useful if it focuses on tracking the results of *particular* education changes undertaken by science and mathematics faculty (e.g., new equipment or software; changes in curriculum content, sequence, or instructional

practices). These assessments should not only identify results, but, in order to be more useful to faculty, should also identify problems encountered and recommend solutions. New projects and other significant SBM-related actions should be linked to school improvement objectives relating to student interest and learning. Site councils should play a greater role in encouraging and sponsoring these evaluations. Science and mathematics faculty can play a major role in designing more "scientifically" sound assessments, possibly involving their students in designing, implementing, and analyzing the findings.

Overall, we did not find dramatic changes or improvements resulting from SBM. However, we did find in those schools and with those faculty members that took advantage of their added flexibility under SBM that numerous small-scale changes and improvements did occur. The concepts of SBM seem sound; successful implementation is difficult. We hope the recommendations presented in this report can help schools improve their implementation efforts.

Use of the term "SBM" (or any other special label) should probably be phased out to avoid giving school staff the feeling that the approach is special or ad hoc ("faddish"). Over the long run, SBM-style decentralization should become a *routine* characteristic of a school. It should become just "the way things are done around here."

Participating Schools and School Districts

APPENDIX A: Participating Schools and School Districts

MIDDLE SCHOOLS

	District Data		School Data								
District/State	District Enrollment	%/# of Schools with SBM	School Name	Grade Levels	Community Type	School Enrollment	# Teachers	Student/Teacher Ratio	# S + M Teachers	Student Demographics[a]	SBM Start Date
Albuquerque, NM	89,900	100% — 11 of 11 HS, 23 of 23 MS, 79 of 79 ES, 5 of 5 Alt. Schools	Roosevelt Middle School	6-8	Suburban	470	35	13:1	S: 4 M: 5	African American:<1% / Caucasian: 64% / Hispanic: 35% / Lunch Subsidy: 22%	1989
Prince William County, VA	45,000	100% — 6 of 6 HS, 11 of 11 MS, 39 of 39 ES	Fred Lynn Middle School	6-8	Suburban	1,080	72	15:1	S: 10 M: 10	African American:24% / Caucasian: 60% / Hispanic: 10% / Lunch Subsidy: 24%	1989
Santa Fe, NM	12,830	100% — 3 of 3 HS, 3 of 3 MS, 19 of 19 ES	Capshaw Middle School	7-8	Suburban	580	38	15:1	S: 3 M: 4	African American: 1% / American Indian: 2% / Caucasian: 51% / Hispanic: 46% / Lunch Subsidy: 28%	1988
Fort Worth, TX	70,000	100% — 14 of 14 HS, 20 of 20 MS, 66 of 66 ES	Morningside Middle School	6-8	Urban	735	45	16:3	S: 4 M: 5	African American:85% / Caucasian: 9% / Hispanic: 6% / Lunch Subsidy: 70%	1984

District		School	Grades	Setting	Enrollment		Ratio	S:/M:	Demographics	Year
Prince George's County, MD	108,000 / 87.8% / 18 of 20 HS / 24 of 26 MS / 101 of 117 ES	Oxon Hill Middle School	7-8	Suburban	544	35	15:1	S: 4 M: 4	African American: 79%, Asian: 10%, Caucasian: 9%, Hispanic: 2%, Lunch Subsidy: 22%	1989
Salt Lake City, UT	25,000 / 100% / 3 of 3 HS / 5 of 5 MS / 27 of 27 ES	Bryant Intermediate School	7-8	Urban	653	29	23:1	S: 3 M:3	African American: 3%, American Indian: 3%, Caucasian: 86%, Hispanic: 8%, Lunch Subsidy: (?)	1989
Bellevue, WA	14,758 / 100% / 5 of 5 HS / 6 of 6 MS / 16 of 16 ES	Highland Middle School	6-8	Urban	691	36	19:1	S:7 M:7	African American: 6%, American Indian: 1%, Asian: 16%, Caucasian: 75%, Hispanic: 4%, Lunch Subsidy: 22%	1988
Dade County, FL	254,235 / 56.4% / 14 of 28 HS / 36 of 48 MS / 99 of 188 ES (149/264)	Miami Springs Middle School	6-8	Urban	1,673	63	26:1	S:8 M:10	African American:15%, Asian: 1%, Caucasian: 14%, Hispanic: 70%, Lunch Subsidy: 61.2%	1988
Hillsborough, FL	120,000 / 26.4% / 1 of 14 HS / 5 of 26 MS / 33 of 108 ES (39/148)	Van Buren Junior High School	7-9	Urban	856	33	25:1	S:6 M:6	African American:42%, Asian: 1%, Caucasian: 47%, Hispanic: 10%, Lunch Subsidy: Free 51%, Reduced 10%	1990

a. Categories are not uniform. They reflect the information supplied by the schools.

HIGH SCHOOLS

District/State	District Data		School Name	School Data							SBM Start Date
	District Enrollment	%/# of Schools with SBM		Grade Levels	Community Type	School Enrollment	# Teachers	Student/Teacher Ratio	# S + M Teachers	Student Demographics[a]	
Albuquerque, NM	89,900	100% 11 of 11 HS 23 of 23 MS 79 of 79 ES 5 of 5 Alt. Schools	Sandia High School	9-12	Suburban	1,865	79	24:1	S:10 M:13	African American: 6% Asian: 6% Caucasian: 69% Hispanic: 19% Lunch Subsidy: eligible 2%	1990
Prince William County, VA	45,000	100% 6 of 6 HS 11 of 11 MS 39 of 39 ES	Woodbridge Senior High School	9-12	Suburban	2,900	400	7:1	S: 20 M: 22	African American: 12% Hispanic: 7%	1988
Santa Fe, NM	12,830	100% 3 of 3 HS 3 of 3 MS 19 of 19 ES	Capital High School	19-12	Urban	1,031	68	15:1	S:6 M:6	African American: 1% American Indian: 0.5% Asian: 0.5% Caucasian: 26% Hispanic: 72%	1988
Adams County Twelve Five Star District, Northglen, CO	21,000	100% 3 of 3 HS 6 of 6 MS 24 of 24 ES	Horizon High School	10-12	Suburban	1,435	78	18:1	S:11 M:10	African American: 1% American Indian: 0.5% Asian: 2% Caucasian: 81.5% Hispanic: 15% Lunch Subsidy: Free 21%	1985

Location	Population	% of Schools	School	Grades	Setting	Enrollment		Ratio	Staff	Demographics	Year
Kalispell, MT	4,500	100% 1 of 1 HS 1 of 1 MS 5 of 5 ES	Flathead High School	10-12	Rural	1,500	93	17:1	S:13 M:12	African American: 1% American Indian/Eskimo: 3% Asian: 1% Caucasian: 93% Hispanic: 2% Lunch Subsidy: 13%	1984
Prince George's County, MD	108,000	87.8% 18 of 20 HS 24 of 26 MS 101 of 117 ES	Northwestern High School	9-12	Suburban	1,850	125	15:1	S:11 M:16	African American: 68.2% American Indian: 0.1% Asian: 4.6% Caucasian: 12.7% Hispanic: 14.5% Lunch Subsidy: 20%	1989
Salt Lake City, UT	25,000	100% 3 of 3 HS 5 of 5 MS 27 of 27 ES	West High School	9-12	Urban	2,024	96	21:1	S:8 M:10	African American: 4.14% American Indian: 1.58% Asian: 5.28% Caucasian: 74.32% Hispanic: 11.95% Pacific Islander: 2.12% Other: 0.44%	1989
Dade County, FL	254,235	56.4% 14 of 28 HS 36 of 48 MS 99 of 188 ES	American Senior High School	9-12	Urban	3,714	143	26:1	S:18 M:21	African American: 31% Caucasian: 13% Hispanic: 56% Lunch Subsidy: 9.5%	1989

HIGH SCHOOLS

District/State	District Data		School Name	Grade Levels	Community Type	School Data					SBM Start Date
	District Enrollment	%/# of Schools with SBM				School Enrollment	# Teachers	Student/Teacher Ratio	# S + M Teachers	Student Demographics	
Hillsborough, FL	120,000	26.4% 1 of 14 HS 5 of 26 MS 33 of 108 ES (139/148)	Plant City High School	10-12	Suburban	2,098	91	23:1	S:15 M:16	African American: 14% Asian: 1% Caucasian: 78% Hispanic: 8% Lunch Subsidy: Free 16% Reduced 3%	1990
Poway, CA	25,000	100% 3 of 3 HS 4 of 4 MS 16 of 16 ES	Rancho Bernardo High School	9-12	Suburban	2,500	93	27:1	S:13 M:14	African American: 3% American Indian: 1% Filipino: 13% Caucasian: 76% Hispanic: 6%	1990

a. Categories are not uniform. They reflect the information supplied by the schools.

APPENDIX B

Literature Review

Prior to our field work, we conducted a review of literature related to school-based management (SBM) and similar educational reforms. The purpose of the initial literature review was to: a) identify elements that should be examined in our study of individual school systems—that is, to provide guidance in developing our research design; and b) provide confirmatory or contradictory evidence to help us make our final recommendations. The review presented here comprises that initial literature review, supplemented by another, brief review conducted after the start of the field work. This additional research incorporated new literature and less-readily available materials that came to light as we performed the various tasks associated with the project.

There is a considerable and growing amount of literature on SBM, and school reform and restructuring. The literature on reform and restructuring is particularly extensive since it incorporates virtually all forms of educational change (school choice, teacher certification, accountability, assessment, etc.). It is difficult, however, to single out material relevant to SBM or other forms of decentralization in the more general educational reform and restructuring literature. Thus, the literature reviewed for this project was primarily restricted to that which focused on SBM. It should be noted that SBM and similar terms are commonly used in the literature, while decentralization—the broader term used in this report—typically is not found.

We first report on general SBM concepts from the literature. This overview is followed by sections on potential implications of SBM for science and mathematics education and factors affecting SBM implementation in science and mathematics education. It should be noted that the literature on SBM and similar reform efforts seldom specifically addresses the implications for science and mathematics education—or for any other subject area. The SBM literature, however, covers issues likely to be applicable to science and mathematics education. We end with a review of the literature implications regarding monitoring and evaluation of SBM efforts.

THE CONCEPT AND GROWTH OF SCHOOL-BASED MANAGEMENT

There are many names and definitions for school-based management, including school-site management, school-based budgeting, school-site autonomy, and shared governance (Clune and White 1988). School restructuring also commonly refers to SBM (Cohen 1988; David et al. 1989; Elmore 1988; Fullan 1993). As Bailey (1991) points out, SBM is about "who is the boss," which affects other key reform issues in education, such as what is taught and how it is taught. Although SBM is defined in a variety of ways (Malen et al. 1989), it is typically described as a change in school governance structure that increases authority at the school site (Clune and White 1988; Malen et al. 1989). In other words, SBM entails decentralization of authority, a broader concept than SBM, that can encompass a variety of efforts and that avoids the "faddishness" of labels such as SBM.

SBM has become a major educational reform movement in elementary and secondary education. The Rutgers-based Center for Policy Research in Education has said that SBM has a "strategic position at the crossroads of major trends in state and local policy" (Clune and White 1988). The National Governors' Association (NGA) has produced three policy papers on SBM since 1988 (Cohen 1988; David et al. 1989; Elmore 1988). These papers followed the NGA task force report "Time for Results: The Governors' 1991 Report on Education" (1986), which (among other things) called for promotion of school-site management. Kentucky has mandated statewide adoption of school-based decision making in its Education Reform Act of 1990, beginning in 1991-92 (to be fully implemented by 1996-97) (Van Meter 1991). The Council of Chief State School Officers (CCSSO 1989) notes that school restructuring has become a major part of national discussions about education, and that teacher unions are among the supporters of decentralized decision making.

Some of the literature (Clune and White 1988; NGA 1986) points out that some of the findings of the effective-schools research, reforms concerned with deregulation and decentralization, and the recommendations of the Carnegie Forum on Education and the Economy are also relevant to SBM. The last calls for restructuring schools to provide a more professional environment for teachers by increasing teacher participation in decision making (Carnegie Forum 1986). Some descriptions of SBM efforts include other characteristics associated with effective-school research, such as expectations that all students can learn, a healthy school atmosphere, and the importance of principal leadership (Burns and Howes 1988; Carr 1988). Schools with SBM also have some of the characteristics associated with "focus schools" (a category encompassing characteristics commonly found in Catholic schools and special-purpose public schools), primarily the ability to initiate action to pursue their missions, solve their own problems, and manage external relations (Hill et al. 1990). The increased school-site autonomy and flexibility of SBM is also a characteristic of the essential-schools concept (Sizer 1984).

There is a growing body of literature that directly or indirectly addresses SBM. SBM is incorporated (specifically or by reference) in the literature on educational reform movements (such as Cuban 1988; Purkey and Smith 1985; Timar and Kirp 1989), as well as the literature on SBM itself. As David (1989) and Malen et al. (1990; 1989) point out, a considerable portion of the SBM literature consists of advocacy pieces, position papers, testimonials, and conceptual guides. Clune and White (1988) and David (1989) note that there is surprisingly little empirical research on SBM. In their literature review, Malen et al. (1990; 1989) identify only eight systematic investigations of SBM based on case studies in a variety of locations, but note these were not comparable because they had examined different versions of SBM and focused on different dimensions. Additional empirical research on SBM is under way, although the number of schools or districts studied remains fairly small (Hallinger et al. 1991; Taylor and Teddlie 1992; Weiss 1992).

Some of the SBM literature focuses on describing how SBM works with respect to what decisions are, or should be, decentralized, and how SBM is, or should be, operationalized (Bailey 1991; Clune and White 1988; David 1989; Prasch 1990; White 1989). Some of the SBM case studies literature also contain descriptions of SBM operations (Casner-Lotto 1988; Clune and White 1988; David et al. 1989; David and Peterson 1984; Fairfax County Public Schools 1986; Sickler 1988).

√ Under SBM, individual schools, their teachers, parents, and sometimes others (such as students, noninstructional personnel, and community representatives) are given increased authority over one or more responsibilities including the school budget, curriculum and instruction, and school staffing. The basic hypothesis is that such decentralization to the school level will stimulate organizational renewal, strengthen school-wide planning, raise the morale and motivation of school staff, stimulate instructional improvement or innovations, foster development of characteristics associated with effective schools, and improve student achievement (Clune 1989; Malen et al. 1990). Since there is no single model of SBM (Clune and White 1988; David 1989; Elmore 1991; Mojkowski and Fleming 1988; Prasch 1990), decisions over all three areas are not necessarily delegated in all instances of SBM, nor is the extent of delegation the same for all three within or across school districts.

√ A good deal of the SBM literature focuses on the supporting rationales or theories underlying the concept, particularly the view that better decisions—that is, decisions leading to better educational outcomes—can be made by those closest to the student/school because they are most aware of the problems and needs at that level (Clune and White 1988; White 1989). This view is supported by groups such as the American Federation of Teachers, the National Educational Association, the National Governors' Association, and studies such as the 1986 Carnegie Task Force on Teaching as a Profession (Conley and Bacharach 1990; White 1989).

A related theme is the importance of participatory management (which is a key feature of SBM) and organizational (i.e., school) culture in designing and implementing educational improvement or reform (Cuban 1988; Conley and Bacharach 1990; Orlich 1989; Sirotnik and Clark 1988; Timar and Kirp 1989). Some of the literature (Carr 1988; Clune and White 1988; Hill et al. 1990; Purkey and Smith 1985) links organizational culture, participatory, flexible management attributes associated with SBM, and similar reforms to the broader organizational excellence theories of Peters and Waterman (1982). Prasch (1990) points out that SBM is consistent with movements toward decentralization and participatory management in business and industry.

Despite generally positive descriptions of the rationale for decentralization, some of the literature raises concerns about SBM's ability to impact education. Elmore (1991) noted that SBM lacks an explicit explanation or theory for translating organizational changes into changes in instructional practice and learning. In addition, new systems (such as SBM) must be implemented within the constraints of existing knowledge and relationships, which may neutralize their effect on the overall performance of schools. Finally, he points out that educational innovations in general are often poorly designed and/or implemented, often without a clear understanding of the processes and institutions they are trying to affect. Fullan (1993) makes a similar point about implementation, noting that rapid implementation of new structures (such as SBM) creates confusion, ambiguity, and conflict, which ultimately may lead to retrenchment. He suggests that an organizational culture conducive to change is needed if restructuring efforts, such as decentralization, are to succeed.

Some of the more recent literature raises additional concerns about SBM's potential to have positive impacts on teaching practices or students learning (Fullan 1993; Hallinger et al. 1991; Taylor and Teddlie 1992; Weiss 1992). A recent study of a small group of teachers and principals indicates that neither group made much of a connection between new governance structures and the teaching-learning process (Hallinger et al. 1991). Taylor and Teddlie (1992) note that early literature on restructuring efforts predicted that changes in teaching practice could be expected, although this area was largely neglected in actual research on restructuring. Their study in one district known for its SBM efforts suggested that teaching practices were not affected by teachers' greater participation in decision making associated with the district's SBM effort.

Similarly, a recent study of 12 high schools across the country—6 with and 6 without formal structures for teacher participation in decision making—found no evidence that such teacher participation increased the schools' focus on curriculum or pedagogy (Weiss 1992). Although the schools with decentralized decision making had adopted more of the current educational reform prescriptions (interdisciplinary teaching, block scheduling, etc.), these changes appeared to be associated with the arrival of a new principal or superintendent with a reform agenda, rather than with the participatory role of teachers. However, shared decision making may have promoted greater teacher support for or "ownership" of such innovations (Weiss 1992).

POTENTIAL IMPLICATIONS FOR SCIENCE AND MATHEMATICS EDUCATION

None of the SBM literature we found focuses on implications of SBM for science and mathematics. Some literature that reports specific examples of changes under SBM includes such examples for science or mathematics (Clune and White 1988; Casner-Lotto 1988; David et al. 1989). One recent article describes the integrated science course developed by science teachers in a restructured high school. The development of this course was consistent with, and supported by, the overall restructuring emphasis in place in that school, although the author did not suggest that its development was a direct result of the restructuring effort (Crane 1991).

Despite their absence of focus on science and mathematics, the discussions in the general SBM literature allow us to extrapolate ways in which SBM could affect science and mathematics education. As noted above, decisions involving the budget, personnel, curriculum, and instruction are typically identified for delegation to the school level under SBM (although the kind and degree of authority delegated can vary considerably in practice). Each of these areas can impact science and mathematics education, as discussed below.

Delegation of *budgeting authority* can entail the authority to allocate funds across a variety of categories according to priorities established at the school level (White 1989) or over a specified amount of discretionary funds (David 1989). For example, each school in the Poway Unified School District determines its own process for deciding how to spend its materials and supplies budget. In some schools, part or all of this budget is divided among the teachers, to be spent according to each teacher's wants; in others, a school-wide committee decides on all expenditures (David et al. 1989).

Increased budget authority at the school level could be used in a variety of ways to affect science and mathematics education. It can translate into the purchase of additional supplies and equipment for science and mathematics teachers or departments—or fewer (especially if the science and mathematics faculty are not able to clearly articulate their needs). Such purchases are particularly important for updating curriculum, texts, and instructional methods; creating a "problem-solving" environment that incorporates technology (such as computers and calculators); or allowing for more experiential learning or "hands-on" experimentation, problem solving, and application that promote student enthusiasm and interest, and encourage the use of reasoning and communication skills (Dossey et al. 1988; Knapp et al. 1988; Lewis 1990; Mullis 1988; National Council of Teachers of Mathematics 1989; Pejouhy 1990; U.S. Congress 1988). Under SBM, a science department might decide, for example, to establish a science equipment and supplies center (similar to a media center). Budget authority also could be used to make it easier for science and mathematics faculty to finance field trips to local industries, laboratories, science museums, planetaria, or environmental sites to provide students with a better understanding of science and mathematics applications.

Budget authority can be used to create staffing flexibility, by enabling the hiring of more science and mathematics teachers, teacher aides, laboratory assistants, or part-time specialists in place of, for example, some administrative or other non-instructional personnel. This kind of flexibility can be particularly important for science and mathematics education, given the acknowledged shortages of qualified science and mathematics teachers (Darling-Hammond et al. 1989; Knapp et al. 1988; National Science Board Commission 1983; National Science Foundation and Department of Education 1980).

Delegation of authority over *staffing decisions* also can be particularly important to science and mathematics education. Some of the ways staffing authority can be used are noted above in the discussion of budget authority. Staffing authority potentially can also be used to provide in-service training or staff development opportunities to strengthen or update science and mathematics teaching abilities. In Dade County, for example, pilot schools in the SBM effort each received $6,250 for staff development, and some teachers in these schools have taken more initiative in requesting specific kinds of training to meet their needs (David et al. 1989). SBM-derived training or staffing flexibility could also facilitate more innovative approaches to science and mathematics training, such as placing teachers in industry or research laboratories (Pallrand 1989).

Other ways schools could strengthen science and mathematics teaching might include establishing a system of mentor or lead teachers (as in Cincinnati and Dade County, among others) to provide peer assistance to new teachers, or developing teaching models or workshops covering specific subjects or teaching approaches, or trying group teaching (as in Hammond, Indiana, and the Thomas Jefferson Science and Technology High School in Fairfax, Virginia) (Casner-Lotto 1988; David et al. 1989; Johnson 1988; MacPhail-Wilcox et al. 1990; Raebeck 1990; Sickler 1988). Science or mathematics mentor teachers would be particularly helpful to teachers who have had relatively little coursework in science and mathematics, or those teaching "out of field."

Greater school staff involvement in making hiring decisions can facilitate the hiring of specialists and aides with science and mathematics qualifications related to specific student needs or gaps in faculty abilities (White 1989). Under SBM, schools might request waivers to hire noncertified teachers (such as scientists, engineers, or mathematicians working in business or industry) to teach classes in their areas of expertise (David et al. 1989), thus exposing students to current applications of science and mathematics.

Delegation of authority in *curriculum and instruction* generally means that teachers are encouraged to develop curriculum, select textbooks, select or create instructional materials, and make changes in instructional methods. These measures can help keep curriculum and texts up to date, which is particularly important in the rapidly changing fields of science and technology. Science or mathematics departments might use staffing authority to assign someone to research recent science and mathematics educational literature for information on current curriculum or current practices in teaching and learning. Science and mathematics teachers have reported needing assistance in obtaining information about instructional materials (National Science Foundation and Department of Education 1980), a function which could also be performed by such a staff position. Science and mathematics teachers might be allowed daily planning time to facilitate instructional improvement, or teams of teachers or lead teachers might be assigned to develop demonstration lessons, instructional materials, or activities (MacPhail-Wilcox et al. 1990; Raebeck 1990). Greater authority over instructional methods might lead to increased use of teaching practices, such as small group learning, and more experiments and hands-on applications of science and mathematics, which may help increase learning and interest in science (National Council of Teachers of Mathematics 1989; Office of Technology Assessment 1988; Scott and Heller 1991).

Under SBM, schools have developed new math textbooks, changed science curricula, incorporated refresher mathematics into an algebra program, and developed peer-tutoring programs to emphasize thinking skills (Clune and White 1988). The increased authority and flexibility provided by SBM enabled a

Hammond, Indiana, high school to develop an alternative mathematics program, featuring small-group instruction, team teaching, and peer tutoring (Casner-Lotto 1988), to help students who did not perform well in the traditional classroom setting. In one of Santa Fe's elementary schools, science (among other selected subjects) is team-taught in first and second grades, as a result of a faculty-developed SBM project (Carnoy and MacDonell 1989). Respondents to a survey on how school-based budgeting in Albuquerque helped meet the needs of individual schools identified some science- and mathematics-related changes, including, at the middle-school level, the purchase of additional science supplies, the addition of a remedial science program and the purchase of texts for it, and the purchase of transitional mathematics texts for a pre-algebra course (Robinson 1987). Instructional scheduling might also be changed under SBM. At Central Park East Secondary School in New York City, staff decided to limit class periods in order to focus on core subjects. As a result, students in grades seven to ten typically have several two-hour blocks of combined mathematics-science instruction each week (O'Neil 1990). SBM has enabled Charles Drew Elementary School in Miami to offer Saturday classes (O'Neil 1990).

SBM could have *indirect impacts* on science and mathematics education. The increased involvement and autonomy of teachers and the increased authority at the school site might make teaching a more attractive profession, thus helping to recruit and retain qualified teachers (Carnegie Forum 1986; Lays 1989; White 1989).

Darling-Hammond (1990) summarizes a number of assumptions underlying educational bureaucratization and the resulting organizational problems that SBM seeks to redress (although she was addressing school restructuring, not SBM per se): a) organizations are most effective when managed top-down—that is, when front-line workers and their customers are divorced from major decisions—thus restricting flexibility; b) tasks will be performed most efficiently if jobs are highly specialized—e.g., teachers in secondary schools should teach the same subject over and over again to large groups of students—thus discouraging subject integration and enrichment; and c) knowledge residing at the top of a bureaucracy can be codified so well in rules and procedures that the workers need only follow orders, which results in highly regulated course requirements, text material, and prescribed curricula that discourage innovation.

FACTORS AFFECTING SBM IMPLEMENTATION IN SCIENCE AND MATHEMATICS EDUCATION

Although there has been very little empirical research reported on SBM, some of the literature mentions factors associated with successful implementation of SBM. Some of these reports are based primarily on a limited number of case studies, as Clune and White (1988) and David and Peterson (1984) point out, while others are primarily based on related research and literature (Conley and Bacharach 1990; Purkey and Smith 1985; White 1989). None of the literature of which we are aware specifically addresses factors relating primarily to science and mathematics. However, the factors identified as affecting SBM implementation in general also appear relevant to SBM's implementation in science and mathematics education.

A key factor associated in the literature with successful implementation of SBM is meaningful involvement of school staff (particularly faculty) in designing and implementing the changes associated with SBM (David et al. 1989; David and Peterson 1984; Purkey and Smith 1985). School staff can be involved early in SBM efforts via the school-level "needs assessment" that is frequently an early step in developing a school's SBM plan (David and Peterson 1984; Purkey and Smith 1985). It thus follows that the extent of science and mathematics faculty participation in SBM efforts is a likely factor in the successful application of SBM for these subjects.

Some of the literature emphasizes that faculty participation in SBM must be "meaningful" or "genuine," and that SBM will not have the desired effects if greater delegation of authority to the school level translates only into more authority for the principal (Clune and White 1988; Conley and Bacharach 1990; David 1989; David and Peterson 1984; Marburger 1985; Purkey and Smith 1985). Duttweiler (1990) suggests that a transformation of authority should be supported by development of a system-wide culture that emphasizes norms of collegiality and collaboration. Fullan (1993) also points out that a culture that supports change—including the beliefs and habits of collaboration and continuous improvement—is needed to support restructuring efforts.

The nature of the role delegated to or adopted by school-level decision-making bodies is also likely to affect the impact of SBM. In a study of SBM implementation in two Minnesota school districts over a four-year period, Jenni (1990) characterized site council activities as being more discussional and observational (receiving information) than advisory and decisional. This failing may have been related to the failure of the school to provide clear information about the extent of authority delegated or to provide training (discussed further below). Underlying factors may have included the unwillingness of the administration to share power or resistance to change. Lindquist and Mauriel (1989) point out that limiting site councils to advisory roles or to "small decisions" is likely to reduce their motivation to continue functioning. However, there may be other reasons for the decisions site councils focus on. Fullan (1993) notes that decentralization efforts may not be as successful as desired because groups get preoccupied with governance issues.

White (1989) mentions that district-level administrators, as well as principals, must be willing to share authority. Others indicate that central (school district, board, or superintendent) support is an important factor in SBM success (Clune and White 1988; David 1989; Lindquist and Mauriel 1989; Marburger 1985; Purkey and Smith 1988; White 1989). The need for central administration units to change roles from decision making to facilitation or support has also been noted (Duttweiler 1990; Harrison et al. 1989; Neal 1988; Prasch 1990). Similarly, existing policies and reporting arrangements may need to be changed because they reflect more centralized control arrangements (Mitchell 1990; Prasch 1990). Fullan (1993) suggests that schools and school districts need to influence each other, continually negotiating the process and agenda of change.

Union support, or at least lack of opposition, is also seen as a key factor in SBM implementation (David et al. 1989; Purkey and Smith 1988; White 1989). Some of the literature notes that provisions for waiving district, state, or union requirements or rules promote SBM success (David 1989; David et al. 1989).

Some factors of success related to delegation of authority were also mentioned in the literature. David and Peterson (1984) note that there must be a core of teachers favorably disposed toward change, in addition to administrative support. Also mentioned was the use of pilot efforts and school self-selection to participate in SBM, to assure that SBM is implemented where there is a favorable school culture or climate for change (David et al. 1989; David and Peterson 1984; Purkey and Smith 1985). A need for leadership, primarily by the principal (or perhaps in the form of an outside liaison or "change agent"), was also seen as a factor for success (David and Peterson 1984; Purkey and Smith 1985).

The literature also mentions a need for clear goals or shared goals and for a clear statement of the nature and degree of authority delegated to various participants (Caldwell and Wood 1988; Hallinger et al. 1991; Harrison et al. 1989; Malen et al. 1990; Prasch 1990; Purkey and Smith 1985; White 1989). Supporting this point was Clune and White's (1988) finding that apprehension and uncertainty related to unclear expectations was a problem in SBM implementation. Rutherford (1991) notes that ambiguity can have a negative impact on development of SBM. Variations in understanding of its meaning make it more difficult to establish a common language and expectations within or among schools, thus making it more difficult to implement.

Prasch (1990) and Caldwell and Wood (1988) point out that information should be shared—both within the school and among the central office and schools—to foster intelligent participation in decision making. Mechanisms for communicating with teachers and others not directly involved with school site councils are also important to SBM success (Aronstein et al. 1990). Some of the literature emphasizes the development of specific planning procedures, including action plans, to guide decision making at the school level (Carr 1988; Caldwell and Wood 1988; Herman 1989; Lytle 1989; Strauber et al. 1990).

Two factors associated with successful SBM implementation that received particular emphasis in the literature were time and resources, such as resources for technical assistance or training, particularly during the early stages of SBM (Clune and White 1988; David et al. 1989; David 1989; Malen et al. 1990; Purkey and Smith 1985; White 1989). Taylor and Teddlie (1992) state that training in topics such as shared decision making and conflict resolution, while important to SBM, is unlikely to affect teaching practices; training in alternative teaching methods is needed if such changes are the desired result of SBM.

One approach to providing technical assistance was to make "change agents" or liaisons available to work with schools implementing SBM (David and Peterson 1984); another was use of planning and implementation grants (Purkey and Smith 1985). In Santa Fe, for example, a foundation grant for technical assistance provides funding for consultants and some trips by teacher representatives to other innovative school districts (Carnoy and MacDonell 1989). Such exposure to practices in other school districts could be particularly valuable in disseminating successful innovations in science and mathematics education. In Chesterfield, Missouri, the school district allocated $75,000 to support team training during the first two years of SBM, and allowed schools to select one or more of three training approaches (or none) (Burns and Howes 1988).

Time needs were defined as allowing time for participants to learn new skills associated with participative management and team building, as well as the time necessary for participation itself (e.g., meetings) (Clune and White 1988; Collins 1990; David 1989; Rutherford 1991). Time to implement SBM also was mentioned. Weiss (1992) points out that schools with shared decision making appeared to spend a considerable amount of time and effort on decisions regarding the decision process itself. While this is to be expected in the early stages of implementation, it also appeared to continue, or recur, several years after SBM went into effect. White (1989) notes that districts with successful SBM programs believed that a gradual transition to SBM helped limit implementation problems. Others (Burns and Howes 1988; David 1989; English 1989; Prasch 1990) point out that implementing SBM and/or seeing results from it takes a long time. The introduction of other innovations at the same time that SBM is being implemented may affect SBM's implementation (Rutherford 1991). Introduction of multiple innovations can affect the amount of time and energy available for each, and may also lead to confusion.

The factors related to SBM implementation discussed above also have implications for SBM implementation in science and mathematics education. Simply introducing SBM in a school does not assure that changes will occur in science and mathematics teaching and learning. Have efforts to increase decision-making authority affected only school-wide issues and decisions made by a site council (which may or may not have science and mathematics teachers as members), or have there been efforts to increase authority in science and mathematics departments? Have mechanisms or procedures been developed to enable science and mathematics teachers to provide input to SBM decision-making bodies or to exercise more authority at the departmental level? [Have science and mathematics teachers received adequate information about SBM and opportunities for increased authority within it, and have they taken advantage of such opportunities? Have science and mathematics teachers received training or been allocated time for involvement in SBM decision making or planning activities?]

MONITORING AND EVALUATION

SBM efforts are frequently accompanied by accountability mechanisms, including school performance reports, monitoring mechanisms such as on-site school review teams (which may involve observation, interviews, and review of written documentation), or reports from principals or other participants (Clune and White 1988; David et al. 1989; David 1989; David and Peterson 1984). Kentucky's planned SBM effort, for example, is accompanied by accountability measures that include the development of performance-based assessment procedures and monetary rewards to successful schools (Van Meter 1991). Some SBM efforts require participating schools to develop plans to meet various kinds of objectives (such as performance objectives, activities to be carried out) and to identify criteria or procedures for determining whether objectives have been obtained (David et al. 1989; David and Peterson 1984). Clune and White (1988) note that monitoring systems sometimes accompany the introduction of SBM programs, but that such systems are not always maintained after the initial stages of the program.

Clune and White (1988) note that there have been few attempts to evaluate the effects of SBM on student outcomes. David et al. (1989) reported that district leaders (in four districts surveyed) were unwilling to predict that test scores would increase in the next few years because these measures are not well matched to the goals of SBM efforts. However, district leaders and individual schools were interested in creating accountability devices suited to the goals of their SBM efforts. Districts and schools also recognized the need for feedback to reflect progress toward goals and for accountability purposes. The overall evaluation of Dade County's SBM effort did include some student outcome measures, such as achievement on standardized test scores, report card results, student attendance, dropout percentages, and suspension percentages (Collins and Hanson 1991).

There is little information on the nature of SBM monitoring and evaluation in the SBM literature. In a few cases, such efforts appear to be fairly extensive. In the Richardson Independent School District in Dallas County, Texas, schools develop annual performance reports that include process and product evaluations related to their strategic plans for improvement (Carr 1988). Dade County developed a three-year project evaluation plan that called for two years of process evaluation (documenting project activities and preliminary attitudes of participants), followed by an outcome evaluation (Collins 1990). The process evaluations include assessments of teacher awareness of, and attitudes toward, SBM, and their opinions about the school climate. The latter involves use of the "Purdue Teacher Opinionnaire," which enables comparisons with test publisher norms. The Dade County process evaluation also includes interviews and surveys of principals to assess the status of school projects and principals' views.

Although the SBM literature does not provide much information on actual monitoring and evaluation efforts, some of it recommends monitoring and evaluation, including specific references to measures that might be used. For example, Guthrie (1986) recommends annual performance reports that would include data on student performance, such as scores and trends on state-administered achievement tests (preferably with comparison data on other students in the district, state, and nation); absentee, dropout, and turnover rates for students; and information on patterns of course enrollment at the secondary level and "downstream" measures of student performance, such as high school grades and rates of college attendance. He also recommends surveys of parents and professional staff on their satisfaction with the school and their views about its strengths and weaknesses.

Lytle (1989) recommends multiple performance indicators related to individual school goals. Purkey and Smith (1985) also recommend multiple measures, including both criterion-referenced and standardized test scores; data on attendance, dropouts, and vandalism; and scales or measures of the quality of school life, organizational climate, and classroom environment. Clearly, the development of science and mathematics performance indicators would be desirable to monitor SBM's implications for science and mathematics education.

Malen et al. (1990) note that since there are no guarantees that SBM will fulfill its promises, schools and districts should conduct continuous, systematic assessments of SBM programs to identify the conditions necessary for SBM to achieve its objectives and improve school performance.

Bibliography

Bibliography

Aronstein, L. W., M. Marlow, and B. Desilets. 1990. "Detours on the Road to Site-Based Management." *Educational Leadership* 47: 61-63.

Bailey, W. J. 1991. *School-Site Management Applied.* Lancaster, PA: Technomic Publishing Co., Inc.

Beers, D. E. 1984. "School-Based Management." Paper presented at the national convention of the National Association of Elementary School Principals, New Orleans, LA: April.

Burns, L., and J. Howes. 1988. "Handing Control to Local Schools." *The School Administrator* 45 (August): 8-10.

Brickley, D., and T. Westerberg. 1990. "Restructuring a Comprehensive High School." *Educational Leadership* 47 (April): 28-31

Caldwell, B. J., and J. M. Spinks. 1988. *The Self-Managing School.* New York, NY: The Falmer Press.

Caldwell, S. D., and F. H. Wood. 1988. "School-Based Improvement—Are We Ready?" *Educational Leadership* 46 (October): 50-53.

Carnegie Forum on Education and the Economy. 1986. *A Nation Prepared: Teachers for the 21st Century.* New York, NY: Carnegie Corporation.

Carnoy, M., and J. MacDonell. 1989. "School District Restructuring in Santa Fe, New Mexico." New Brunswick, NJ: Center for Policy Research in Education.

Carr, R. A. 1988. "Second-Wave Reforms Crest at Local Initiative." *The School Administrator* 45 (August): 16-18.

Casner-Lotto, J. 1988. "Expanding the Teacher's Role: Hammond's School Improvement Process." *Phi Delta Kappan* 69 (January): 349-53.

CCSSO. 1989. "Success for All in a New Century: A Report by the Council of Chief State School Officers on Restructuring Education." Washington, DC: Council of Chief State School Officers.

Cistone, P. J., J. A. Fernandez, and P. L. Tornillo, Jr. 1989. "School-Based Management/Shared Decision Making in Dade County (Miami)." *Education and Urban Society* 21 (August): 393-402.

Chubb, J. E. 1988. "Why the Current Wave of School Reform Will Fail." *The Public Interest* 90: 28-49.

Clune, W. 1989. "Choice and Control in American Education—Part II: Practice." *Lafollete Policy Report* II (Fall/Winter): 6-11.

Clune, W. H., and P. A. White. 1988. "School-Based Management: Institutional Variation, Implementation, and Issues for Further Research." New Brunswick, NJ: Center for Policy Research in Education.

Cohen, M. 1988. "Restructuring the Education System: Agenda for the 1990s." Washington, DC: National Governors' Association.

Collins, R. A. 1990. "Interim Evaluation Report: School-Based Management/Shared Decision-Making Project: 1988-89, Project-Wide Findings." Miami, FL: Dade County Public Schools Office of Program Evaluation.

Collins, R. A., and M. K. Hanson. 1991. "Summative Evaluation Report: School-Based Management/Shared Decision-Making Project, 1987-88 Through 1989-90." Miami, FL: Dade County Public Schools Office of Program Evaluation.

Conley, S. C., and S. B. Bacharach. 1990. "From School-Site Management to Participatory School-Site Management." *Phi Delta Kappan* 71: 539-44.

Crane, S. 1991. "Integrated Science in a Restructured High School." *Educational Leadership* 49: 39-41.

Cuban, L. 1988. "A Fundamental Puzzle of School Reform." *Phi Delta Kappan* 69 (January): 341-44.

Dade County. 1989. "School-Based Management/Shared Decision-Making." Miami, FL: Dade County Public Schools Office of Program Evaluation.

Darling-Hammond, L. 1990. "Achieving Our Goals: Superficial or Structural Reforms?" *Phi Delta Kappan* 72: 286-95.

Darling-Hammond, L., L. Hudson, and S. N. Kirby. 1989. "Redesigning Teacher Education: Opening the Door for New Recruits to Science and Mathematics Teaching." Santa Monica, CA: RAND Corporation.

David, J. L. 1989. "Synthesis of Research on School-Based Management." *Educational Leadership* 47 (May): 45-53.

David, J. L., and S. M. Peterson. 1984. "Can Schools Improve Themselves? A Study of School-Based Improvement Programs." Palo Alto, CA: Bay Area Research Group.

David, J. L., S. Purkey, and P. White. 1989. "Restructuring in Progress: Lessons From Pioneering Districts." Washington, DC: National Governors' Association.

Dossey, J. A., I. V. Mullis, M. M. Lindquist, and D. L. Chambers. 1988. "The Mathematics Report Card: Are we Measuring Up?" Princeton, NJ: Educational Testing Service.

Duttweiler, P.C. 1990. "Recommendations for Implementing School-Based Management/Shared Decision Making." In *Insights on Educational Policy and Practice*, No. 21. Austin, TX: Southwest Educational Development Laboratory.

Elmore, R. F. 1988. "Early Experiences in Restructuring Schools: Voices from the Field." Washington, DC: National Governors' Association.

_____. 1991. "Innovation in Education Policy." Paper presented at the Conference on Fundamental Questions of Innovation, Governor's Center at Duke University, Durham, NC, May 3-5.

English, F.W. 1989. "School-Site Management." *The Practitioner* XVI (December): 1-6.

Fairfax County Public Schools. 1986. "School-Based Management: A Process for School Improvement." Falls Church, VA: Fairfax County Public Schools Office of Research and Evaluation.

Fullan, M. 1993. "Innovation, Reform and Restructuring Strategies." In *Challenges and Achievements of American Education: The 1993 ASCD Yearbook*, 116-33. Alexandria, VA: Association for Supervision and Curriculum Development.

Ginsberg, R., and B. Berry. 1990. "Experiencing School Reform: The View from South Carolina." *Phi Delta Kappan* 71 (March): 549-52.

Glickman, C. D. 1990. "Pushing School Reform to a New Edge: The Seven Ironies of School Empowerment." *Phi Delta Kappan* 72 (September): 68-75.

Goodlad, J. I. 1984. *A Place Called School*. New York, NY: McGraw-Hill.

Greene, D., and J. L. David. 1984. "A Research Design for Generalizing from Multiple Case Studies." *Evaluation and Program Planning* 7: 73-84.

Guthrie, J. W. 1986. "School-Based Management: The Next Needed Education Reform." *Phi Delta Kappan* 68 (December): 305-309.

Hallinger, P., J. Murphy, and C. Hausman. 1991. "Conceptualizing School Restructuring: Principals' and Teachers' Perceptions." Paper presented at the annual meeting of the American Educational Research Association, Chicago, IL, April.

Harrison, C. R., J. P. Killion, and J. F. Mitchell. 1989. "Site-Based Management: The Realities of Implementation." *Educational Leadership* 46 (May): 55-58.

Hatry, H. P., M. Alexander, and J. R. Fountain, Jr. 1989. *Service Efforts and Accomplishments Reporting: Its Time Has Come for Elementary and Secondary Education.* Norwalk, CT: Governmental Accounting Standards Board.

Herman, J. J. 1989. "A Decision-Making Model: Site-Based Communications/Governance Committees." *NASSP Bulletin* 73 (December): 60-66.

_____. 1990. "School-Based Management: A Checklist of Things to Consider." *NASSP Bulletin* 74 (September): 67-71.

Hill, P. T., and J. Bonan. 1991. "Decentralization and Accountability in Public Education." Santa Monica, CA: RAND Corporation.

Hill, P. T., G. E. Foster, and T. Gendler. 1990. "High Schools with Character." Santa Monica, CA: RAND Corporation.

Huberman, A. M., and M. B. Miles. 1984. *Innovation Up Close.* New York, NY: Plenum Press.

Jenni, R. W. 1990. "Application of the School Based Management Process Development Model." Paper presented at the annual meeting of the American Educational Research Association, Boston, MA, April.

Johnson, S. M. 1988. "Pursuing Professional Reform in Cincinnati." *Phi Delta Kappan* 69 (June): 746-51.

Knapp, M. S., M. S. Stearns, M. St. John, and A. A. Zucker. 1988. "Prospects for Improving K-12 Science Education from the Federal Level." *Phi Delta Kappan* 69: 677-83.

Kolderie, T. 1988. "School-Site Management: Rhetoric and Reality." Minneapolis, MN: Center for Policy Studies (mimeo).

Lays, J. 1989. "Who's in Charge, Anyhow?" *State Legislatures* (October): 14-17.

Levin, H. M. 1991. "Building School Capacity for Effective Teacher Empowerment: Applications to Elementary Schools With At-Risk Students." Paper presented at the annual meeting of the American Educational Research Association, Chicago, IL, April.

Lewis, A. C. 1990. "Getting Unstuck: Curriculum as a Tool of Reform." *Phi Delta Kappan* 71 (March): 534-38.

Lindquist, K. M., and J. J. Mauriel. 1989a. "Depth and Breadth in Innovation Implementation: The Case of School-Based Management." In *Research on the Management of Innovation*, edited by Van de Ven, et al. Cambridge, MA: Harper & Row.

_____. 1989b. "School-Based Management: Doomed to Failure?" *Education and Urban Society* 21 (August): 403-16.

Louis, K. S. 1981. "External Agents and Knowledge Utilization: Dimensions for Analysis and Action." In *Improving Schools: Using What We Know*, edited by R. Lehming and M. Kane. Beverly Hills, CA: Sage Publications.

Lytle, J. H. 1989. "School Site Strategic Planning to Improve District Performance." Paper presented at the annual meeting of the American Educational Research Association, San Francisco, CA: March.

MacPhail-Wilcox, B., R. Forbes, and B. Parramore. 1990. "Project Design: Reforming Structure and Process." *Educational Leadership* 47: 22-25.

Malen, B. and R. T. Ogawa. 1988. "Professional-Patron Influence on Site-Based Governance Councils: A Confounding Case Study." *Educational Evaluation and Policy Analysis* 10 (Winter): 251-70.

Malen, B., R. T. Ogawa, and J. Kranz. 1989. "What Do We Know About School-Based Management? A Case Study of the Literature—A Call for Research." Paper prepared for Conference on Choice and Control in American Education, Madison, WI, May 17-19.

_____. 1990. "Evidence Says Site-Based Management Hindered by Many Factors." The School Administrator 47 (February): 30-32; 53-59.

Marburger, C. 1985. *One School at a Time: School-Based Management—A Process for Change*. Columbia, MD: National Committee for Citizens in Education.

Mauriel, J. J. 1988. "Rationale for Decentralized (Site) Management in Public Schools." Advanced Management Practices Paper #5, Strategic Management Research Center, University of Minnesota (mimeo), Minneapolis, MN.

McClure, R. M. 1988. "The Evolution of Shared Leadership." *Educational Leadership* 46: 60-62.

McWalters, P. 1992. "Handing Accountability and Authority to Schools." *The School Administrator* 49: 9-10.

Meadows, B. J. 1990. "The Rewards and Risks of Shared Leadership." *Phi Delta Kappan* 71 (March): 545-48.

Miles, M. B., and A. M. Huberman. 1984. *Qualitative Data Analysis: A Sourcebook of New Methods*. Beverly Hills, CA: Sage Publications.

Mitchell, J. E. 1990. "Coaxing Staff from Cages for Site-Based Decisions to Fly." *The School Administrator* 47 (February): 23-26.

Mojkowski, C., and D. Fleming. 1988. "School-Site Management: Concepts and Approaches." Cranston, RI: Rhode Island Educational Leadership Academy (mimeo).

Montgomery County Public Schools. 1991. "The Flexibility Pilot: Shared Decision-Making in Selected Montgomery County Public Schools." Rockville, MD: Montgomery County Public Schools.

Mullis, I. V. S., and L. B. Jenkins. 1988. "The Science Report Card: Elements of Risk and Recovery." Princeton, NJ: Educational Testing Service.

National Council of Teachers of Mathematics. 1989. *Curriculum and Evaluation Standards for School Mathematics*. Reston, VA: The National Council of Teachers of Mathematics.

National Governors' Association. 1986. "Time for Results: The Governors' 1991 Report on Education." Washington, DC: National Governors' Association.

National Science Board Commission on Precollege Education in Mathematics, Science and Technology. 1983. "Educating Americans for the 21st Century." Washington, DC: National Science Board Commission.

National Science Foundation and the Department of Education. 1980. *Science and Engineering Education for the 1980s and Beyond*. Washington, DC: U.S. Government Printing Office.

Neal, R. 1988. "School Based Management: An Advanced Model." Paper presented at the annual meeting of the Association of Negotiators and Contract Administrators, San Francisco, CA: November.

Newman, F. M. 1991. "Linking Restructuring to Authentic Student Achievement." *Phi Delta Kappan* 72 (February): 458-63.

O'Neil, J. O. 1990. "Piecing Together the Restructuring Puzzle." *Educational Leadership* 47: 4-10.

Orlich, D. C. 1989. "Education Reforms: Mistakes, Misconceptions, Miscues." *Phi Delta Kappan* 70 (March): 512-17.

Pallrand, J. 1989. "Science, Technology, and Public Knowledge." *Phi Delta Kappan* 70: 460-64.

Patton, M. Q. 1980. *Qualitative Evaluation Methods*. Beverly Hills, CA: Sage Publications.

Pejouhy, N. H. 1990. "Teaching Math for the 21st Century." *Phi Delta Kappan* 72: 76-78.

Peters, T., and R. Waterman, Jr. 1982. *In Search of Excellence: Lessons from America's Best-Run Companies*. Cambridge, MA: Harper & Row.

Porter, A. 1988. "Indicators: Objective Data or Political Tool?" Phi Delta Kappan 69 (March): 503-508.

Prasch, A. 1990. *How to Organize for School-Based Management.* Alexandria, VA: Association for Supervision and Curriculum Development.

Prince William County Public Schools. 1990. *School-Based Management: Executive Summary.* Manassas, VA: Prince William County Public Schools.

Purkey, S. C., and M. S. Smith. 1985. "School Reform: The District Policy Implications of the Effective Schools Literature." *Elementary School Journal* 85 (January): 353-89.

Raebeck, B. S. 1990. "Transformation of a Middle School." *Educational Leadership* 47: 18-21.

Raywid, M. A. 1990. "The Evolving Effort to Improve Schools: Pseudo-Reform, Incremental Reform, and Restructuring." *Phi Delta Kappan* 72 (October): 139-43.

Robblee, K. M. 1991. "Cooperative Chemistry: Make a Bid for Student Involvement." *The Science Teacher* 58: 20-23.

Robinson, C. 1988. "School-Based Budgeting Survey Study of Pilot Schools." Albuquerque, NM: Albuquerque Public Schools (mimeo).

Romberg, T. A. 1983. "School Mathematics: Options for the 1990s." Chairman's Report of a Conference. Washington, DC: U.S. Department of Education.

Rosenblum, S., and K. S. Louis. 1981. *Stability and Change: Innovation in an Educational Context.* New York, NY: Plenum Press.

Rutherford, B. 1991. "School-Based Management and School Improvement: How it Happened in Three School Districts." Paper presented at the annual meeting of the American Educational Research Association, Chicago, IL, April 3-7.

Saint Louis Public Schools. 1988. "Status Report, Needs Analysis and Recommendations for Full Implementation of School Based Management." St. Louis, MO: St. Louis Public Schools (mimeo).

_____. 1990. "School Based Management: Annual Report 1989-1990." St. Louis, MO: St. Louis Public Schools (mimeo).

Saint Paul Public Schools. 1990. "School Based/Shared Decision Making: An Interim Report to the Professional Issues Committee." St. Paul, MN: Saint Paul Public Schools.

_____. 1991. "Report on School Based Shared Decision Making from the Professional Issues Committee." St. Paul, MN: Saint Paul Public Schools.

Sambs, C. E., and R. Schenkat. 1990. "One District Learns About Restructuring." *Educational Leadership* 7 (April): 72-75.

Santa Fe Public Schools. 1990. "Santa Fe Schools Improvement Program: 1989-90 Annual Report." Santa Fe, NM: Santa Fe Public Schools (mimeo).

Schneider, G. T. 1984. "Teacher Involvement in Decision Making: Zones of Acceptance, Decision Conditions, and Job Satisfaction." *Journal of Research and Development in Education* 18: 25-32.

Sheive, L. T. 1988. "New Roles for Administrators in Rochester." *Educational Leadership* 46 (November): 53-55.

Sickler, J. L. 1988. "Teachers in Charge: Empowering the Professionals." *Phi Delta Kappan* 69 (January): 354-76.

Sirotnik, K. A., and R. W. Clark. 1988. "School-Centered Decision Making and Renewal." *Phi Delta Kappan* 69 (May): 660-64.

Sizer, T. R. 1984. *Horace's Compromise: The Dilemma of the American High School*. Boston, MA: Houghton Mifflin Company.

Strauber, S. K., S. Stanley, and C. Wagenknecht. 1990. "Site-Based Management at Central-Hower." *Educational Leadership* 47 (April): 64-66.

Taylor, D., and C. Teddlie. 1992. "Restructuring and the Classroom: A View from a Reform District." Paper presented at the annual meeting of the American Educational Research Association, San Francisco, CA.

Timar, T. B., and D. L. Kirp. 1989. "Education Reform in the 1980s: Lessons from the States." *Phi Delta Kappan* 70 (March): 504-11.

U. S. Congress, Office of Technology Assessment. 1988. *Elementary and Secondary Education for Science and Engineering; A Technical Memorandum.* Washington, DC: U.S. Government Printing Office.

U. S. General Accounting Office. 1989. *Effective Schools Programs: Their Extent and Characteristics.* Washington, DC: U.S. Government Printing Office.

Van Meter, E. J. 1991. "The Kentucky Mandate: School-Based Decision Making." *NASSP Bulletin* 75: 52-62.

Weiss, C. 1992. "Shared Decision Making About What?" Paper presented at the annual meeting of the American Educational Research Association, San Francisco, CA, April.

White, P. A. 1988. "Resource Materials on School-Based Management." New Brunswick, NJ: Center for Policy Research in Education.

_____. 1989. "An Overview of School-Based Management: What Does the Research Say?" *NASSP Bulletin* 73 (September): 1-8.

Yin, R. K. 1984. *Case Study Research: Design and Methods.* Beverly Hills, CA: Sage Publications.